JOHN BAILEY'S
COMPLETE GUIDE TO
FRESHWATER
FISHING

JOHN BAILEY'S
COMPLETE GUIDE TO
FRESHWATER FISHING

THE FISH, THE TACKLE & THE TECHNIQUES

NEW HOLLAND

First published in 2004 by New Holland Publishers (UK) Ltd
London • Cape Town • Sydney • Auckland

2 4 6 8 10 9 7 5 3 1

www.newhollandpublishers.com

Garfield House, 86-88 Edgware Road, London W2 2EA, United Kingdom

80 McKenzie Street, Cape Town 8001, South Africa

14 Aquatic Drive, Frenchs Forest, NSW 2086, Australia

218 Lake Road, Northcote, Auckland, New Zealand

ISBN 1 84330 567 4

Publishing Manager: Jo Hemmings
Senior Editor: Kate Michell
Copy Editor: Ian Whitelaw
Assistant Editor: Rose Hudson
Designer: Andrew Easton
Production: Joan Woodroffe
Index: Dorothy Frame

Reproduction by Pica Digital Pte Ltd, Singapore
Printed and bound by Kyodo Printing Co (Singapore) Pte Ltd

CONTENTS

INTRODUCTION

I TRULY HOPE THAT THIS BOOK WILL OFFER YOU NOT ONLY PLENTY OF HARD INFORMATION AND ADVICE BUT ALSO INSPIRATION. TO BE A GOOD ANGLER, YOU NOT ONLY NEED TO KNOW HOW TO FISH BUT YOU MUST ALSO WANT PASSIONATELY TO DO IT. IN THE PAGES THAT FOLLOW, AS WELL AS LEARNING HOW TO PURSUE FRESHWATER FISH, I HOPE YOU'LL BE ENTHUSED TO GET OUT THERE AND CATCH THEM.

I believe passionately in fishing for, in truth, it's given me the best times of my life. As a child, fishing fuelled my dreams, and I've been fortunate to live them out as an adult. So many memories…

… a huge carp in the heat of a midsummer day. The lake and its surroundings were like a cauldron, the sweat coursed down my forehead and down my back. For 40 minutes I was unable to move, to swat at the wasp around my head or beat off the horsefly from my thigh. The enormous carp that I'd pursued for three years was hanging like a great purple barge just a hand's span from my bait. I knew he knew there was something wrong. He knew I knew, and after all that excruciating time, he moved off, his bulk raising the water in front of him, his fins stirring the silt as he went. That was my one chance. I never had another, and in a strange way I am pleased. The dream continues.

… my first pike over 30 pounds, caught at 150 yards range on a drifted dead trout. It was a gloomy day, all mists and drizzle, and when the float went down and I struck only to find that I'd hooked the bottom, my spirits were as dark as the winter sky. That is, until the rod began to corkscrew in my hands, until the clutch gave under a mounting, unrelenting pressure. Will I ever forget how the line began to lift all that way from the bank to the middle of the lake, and this huge, angry pike lashed out, balancing on its tail, shaking its flared head from side to side? Can I ever forget the drama of the next 45 minutes as, turn by turn, I finally got line back on the spool until the pike was all but beaten below me, boring in the deep, clear water at my feet like some creature from the age of the dinosaurs?

… my first three-pound roach, swirling in the torch-light as the river made its way through the oozing,

spring marshland landscape. The way it loomed in the landing net that night, impossibly large, awesomely magnificent.

… my first big barbel, all quivering muscle and fins of coral and tangerine, and far beyond my ability to adequately describe.

… the beginnings of my travels abroad. The heat and dust of India, the mahseer of the Himalayan foothills that can empty a reel of line faster than any other fish that lives in fresh water. Following a mahseer down three-quarters of a mile of white, foaming rapids – swimming, bouncing, praying.

… the battle with that exotic salmonid species, the taimen, in Mongolia. For three hours I chased one down two miles of the wildest river in Asia. I'd overcome every problem, survived every danger and it looked impossible that I would lose him – but I did, in water less than knee-deep. As the sun finally sank behind the snow-capped hills to the west, the hooks pulled and the fish simply melted into the gold.

Dusks and dawns, rivers aglow, lakes shrouded in mists. The multitude of fine people I've met along the way, the incredible world of water that I've been privileged to enjoy: the kingfishers, the hunched-up heron, the water hens, the elegant grebes, the whirling mayflies, the fox at dawn and the badger at night. It is fishing that has brought all these into my life, and I'm grateful for it.

➤ A SOFT LANDING
Kerry gently holds up a beautiful barbel for a brief moment in the sunlight. The fish is held over a bed of grass sprouting from shallow water to ensure a soft landing should it wriggle free. In hot sunlight, only take a fish out of water for the minimum possible time and only if absolutely necessary.

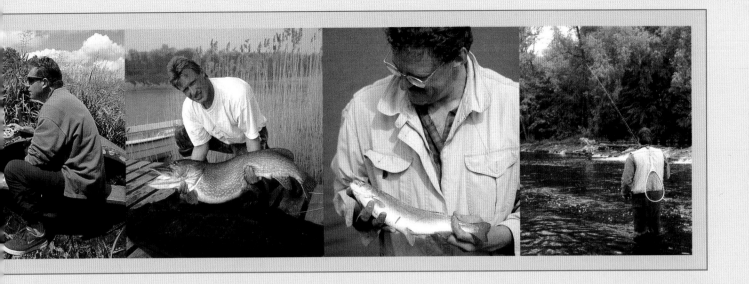

Confidence and Responsibility

I would like to say two things before you begin to take this book on board. It's full of advice that I've gleaned from true experts over the past 40 years, and it should prove to be a tremendous springboard to you becoming a very good angler, but I want to stress that the important thing is to build up your own experience. It's important to realize that there are no such things as absolute rules in fishing. Build up your own personal confidence. Have the independence to see every water and every fishing situation through your own eyes. Don't be afraid to do new things that may seem totally wacky to those around you – it's doing it your own way that counts.

The second thing I want to stress is the importance of doing it right. Bear in mind that to be an angler is a privilege. I won't insult you by imploring you to take away litter, shut gates and the like. I realize that you will do all those things instinctively already. No, I'd rather urge you to think much more deeply about how you approach each and every session on the waterside. Think carefully about the fish and your impact on them. Explore ways in which you can make the catching less stressful for them and more challenging and enjoyable for you.

◀ GETTING OUT THERE

I can't overstress the advantages of wading, but you do need clear, comparatively shallow water to wade in safety. Wear Polaroids to help you pinpoint any snags or drop-offs and never wade out of your depth in a strong current or where you feel in any danger. If you go slowly, without splashing, you can get incredibly close to the fish that you're hunting.

▽ THE BIG MOMENT

Two friends help each other out at the crucial moment. This fine barbel was taken float fishing and both men were wading. Often, holding a float back is the best way to fool suspicious fish. This way the bait rises a little from the bottom and is the very first thing that the fish see.

THE CARING ANGLER'S CODE

- Use barbless hooks or flatten the barbs before fishing. It makes hook removal 10 times easier.
- Try to do without treble hooks as much as possible, even on spinners. They can do untold damage, especially when used in pairs.
- Always wet your hands before touching a fish.
- If at all possible, unhook the fish in the water and let it swim free without ever leaving its own environment.
- If you do have to bring a fish into the air and onto the land, make sure it's kept in a wet landing net or put on an unhooking mat, but never left to writhe on hard gravel or stone or on a sandy beach.
- Never lift a fish by the tail. This will disrupt its skeletal structure and condemn it to a lingering death.
- Only weigh and photograph important specimens. If you do need to do so, make sure each function is carried out on the waterline itself. Keep a very careful check on the amount of time each exercise is taking.
- If a fish is tired after its struggle, support it in the shallows with its head facing upriver so that oxygen can pass through its gills. Do not move the fish backwards and forwards believing this will help the flow of water through its mouth. All you're doing is causing it further distress. Let the fish breathe naturally; in its own time the fish will swim away comfortably.
- The only place for a keep net is in a match-fishing situation.
- Don't be greedy. If you can, catch a couple of fish from a shoal and move on to another challenge. Once you've caught enough fish, pack it in for the day. Remember that fish feel mental stress as well as physical hurt.
- Fishing is a sport in which you can take pride. Let's be proud of ourselves and the way we play it.

# PREPARATION

A LOT OF YOUR BEST WORK IS DONE AT HOME, IN THE TACKLE SHOP
OR ON THE BANKSIDE BEFORE YOU'VE EVEN PUT IN ANY BAIT OR
TACKLE. IT'S ABSOLUTELY ESSENTIAL THAT YOU WORK OUT CLEARLY
IN YOUR MIND THE RIGHT APPROACH FOR EACH AND EVERY FISHING
SITUATION BEFORE YOU BEGIN TO PUT YOUR PLANS INTO ACTION.

KNOWING THE FISH

IN THE WORLD OF FISHING YOU CAN KNOW EVERYTHING THERE IS
TO KNOW ABOUT TACKLE, BAITS AND TECHNIQUES, BUT IF YOU DON'T
UNDERSTAND THE FISH YOU'RE HUNTING THEN NONE OF THESE
COUNTS FOR MUCH. FOR A FISHERMAN, THE FISH IS EVERYTHING. IT'S
HIS FOCUS, HIS WORLD, HIS TOTAL OBJECTIVE. GET TO KNOW THE
FISH, THINK LIKE THE FISH AND YOU'LL START CATCHING THE FISH.

The first thing that we've got to establish is that being a fish is quite unlike being a human being. We both possess that spark of life, but beyond that the differences are almost unbridgeable. It needs a great leap of imagination on our part to understand just how fish lead their lives. Foremost, we have to be aware of the factors that govern the lives of fish: most of these are to do with the natural elements from which we've so carefully insulated ourselves with clothing, central heating and the like. The fish is totally unlike us in this respect: it remains almost entirely at the mercy of the elements, utterly dependent on the conditions that surround it.

The Influence of the Weather
The weather is fundamental to how the fish leads its life at any particular time. In large part this is to do with water temperature. If the air is freezing cold then, obviously, waters will begin to cool down rapidly, too. As a fish is a cold-blooded creature and its body temperature changes with external conditions, the colder the water, in general, the less the fish will want to move around and feed. As a basic rule, therefore, cold and cooling water is the least productive for the angler's efforts. Warm water or warming water tends, generally, to be more conducive to success.

Naturally, there are exceptions: some fish, such as pike or grayling, are well used to cold temperatures and after a short time will happily begin to feed in them. At the other end of the scale, water that is too hot can prove a problem: oxygen levels decrease and fish become ever more lethargic.

The weather affects fish in other ways, too: fish like to know where they are and they enjoy leading ordered, stable lives. For this reason, the majority of fish like periods of high pressure when the weather doesn't change much and water conditions remain fairly constant from day to day. The arrival of a weather front, however, signals change and this can often put fish off the feed until they have learnt to adapt to the new conditions.

Once again, however, there are exceptions: in a period of stifling, hot weather the appearance of wind and rain can beat oxygenated life into previously stagnant ponds. A thunderstorm, too, can galvanize fish.

➤ IN THE BLEAK MIDWINTER
Always think really carefully about the effect that the weather is having on fish movements. Winter high pressure with severe night frosts and daytime temperatures barely creeping above freezing push fish into all the places they can find a little extra warmth. Big beds of rushes, as seen here, tend to leak out heat in the very coldest of weather.

➤ BE GENTLE
Knowing your fish is realizing that they don't like to be taken out of the water, so don't do it more than is absolutely necessary. If possible, simply draw a fish to you, hold it in the current and flick the hook free with a pair of forceps. This is not a big chub, so a quick study like this is all I need. In a second it is on its way.

ᴧ WINTER FEEDING FRENZY

Winter is far from being a complete write off for fishing. If the water temperature is stable or begins to rise and the weather is mild and damp, then fish of all species, which have been fasting and lying dormant for days or weeks, can go on the rampage. Here you see carp throwing up sheets of bubbles in the vicinity of overhanging branches. Another tip: winter carp don't venture far from cover.

In winter, a warm westerly weather front can also raise water temperatures and bring reluctant fish back onto the feed.

So, as you can see, everything has to be considered and taken in context. Just how will every type of weather or change in the weather affect your fishery and the fish within it?

Water on the Move

One of the most important aspects of the weather regarding any fish is rain. Too much rain and, of course, rivers can rise, break their banks and render fishing impossible. For the most part, however, a certain amount of rain is a good thing. In the summer, especially, it can bring fresh, much-needed oxygen into low, drying lakes. Above

all, rain will frequently cloud the water, reducing the visibility. This has two main beneficial effects for the angler. In the first place, cloudy water spells food to the fish and they become invigorated. Secondly, murky water helps mask the deficiencies of any angler's presentation. Put simply, the fish find it more difficult to make out our line and tackle in cloudy water than in clear water. When plenty of rain clouds the water, the odds swing to our side.

Fish are also very dependent on currents within the water. You might think that currents only occur in rivers, but you'd be wrong. The larger the stillwater, the stronger the underwater currents created by the prevailing winds. Fish will often

◄ THE RIVER MENU
Of course, you know that fish don't eat luncheon meat, cheese or bread flake in the wild. So, it's worth digging around in the river and turning up stones to see what the fish are actually eating. Many natural food items can be used on the hook to great effect. The very best of these, in my view, is the caddis grub. Break one out of its protective shell of sand, stone or weed and you have a killing bait for most non-predatory fish.

You'll be amazed at the amount and variety of food items you come across – shrimps, snails, water fleas, leeches, caddis grubs, tiny fish, beetles… the list seems never-ending. Perhaps you'll even stumble across bigger food items such as bullheads and crayfish, ideal bait for barbel, chub or carp. Remember that your unnatural bait will always be competing with these natural food items and that the richer the water, the less need there is for the fish to switch its diet. .

station themselves against the current, making use of the oxygen that it brings. They'll also travel on currents because they expend less energy that way. Vitally, currents also bring food to fish and save them the hassle and energy of digging for it or searching far and wide.

The Vital Ingredient
Food supplies are essential to every living being and, unlike us, fish can't wander down to the local convenience store to be satisfied. Food is arguably any fish's most important consideration. They can put up with a certain amount of discomfort, but alleviating hunger is critical to their success as a species. Fish soon learn their way around their environment.

➤ THE BIG BOYS
Fish also like to gorge on nymphs: the bigger the fish, the greater their liking for giant nymphs. Dragonfly nymphs, damselfly nymphs and stonefly nymphs are all sought after by bottom-feeding species. You'd be surprised, too, how often a hatch of flies brings on a frantic feeding search among river species. So, get in tune with the natural flow of the water you're fishing and see your results improve.

They know which parts of any lake or river are likely to be food rich at any particular time of the year. They're also very quick to harvest any seasonal or unexpected bonus: the mayfly hatch, for example, is enjoyed not only by trout but also by all species of cyprinids (the carp family).

After a heavy rain, have you any idea how many lobworms are washed into the river from the surrounding land? It's an absolute feast for all fish. Go to any river, stand in the shallows and turn over the marginal rocks.

Think about the times the fish feed most during any 24-hour cycle: more insects are drifting in the current during the hours of darkness, and in many waters this is why several species become particularly active after dusk. Also, in the summer especially, a slight dip in the water temperature can stimulate the appetite. This doesn't

mean to say that daytime feeding doesn't happen, because it does, but it's likely to be more opportunistic, making use of a short-lived and perhaps unexpected food bonus.

Ways of Living

Different types of fish lead different lifestyles. At its most simple, we can think of fish as grazers and predators, sheep and wolves. The sheep – generally the carp family in many of our waters – feed fairly constantly, looking to build up a diet of many, many small food items. Carp, tench, roach, bream and the like spend a large proportion of every day feeding slowly and steadily, earning their living with thousands of small food items. The wolves are the predators – the pike, the zander, the big perch, eels or catfish. These are ambush experts, creatures looking to make one big kill that can last them for hours, days or even weeks, depending on the water temperature and the rate of their digestion.

Fish are consequently very concerned about their safety. As eggs and when newly hatched, they are prey to virtually every living thing in their environment – including their parents! As fry and fingerlings, they can be picked off by bigger fish, waterfowl and even dragonfly nymphs. As small fish they are prey for the perch, pike, grebes and cormorants. Even as large fish they're not safe – otters have been known to hunt 20-pound fish.

⋏ ON THE PROWL
You can tell a great deal about the mood of predators from their body language. Pike are a perfect example: when they begin to move up through the layers of water then they're on the prowl, stirred by hunger.

⋎ FEEDING HARD
If you see carp moving slowly along the bottom then they're probably feeding. Look for them tipping up so that the tail rises in the water, forcing the head into the silt and gravel where they can dig for food.

Life beneath the surface is arbitrary and painful, and fish will do everything in their power to increase their chances of survival. They'll swim in shoals, for example, as this increases their chances of survival during a predatory attack. They'll seek out snags, such as fallen branches, and underwater structures, such as boulders and drop-offs, that give them shelter. They'll be wary of thin, clear water and areas of bright light where they can be spotted from above. They'll prefer the shelter of reeds or lily beds, for example. Cloudy water also attracts them, as they become less visible there.

⅄ IN THE JUNGLE
The more fish are pursued, the more they search for refuge. Fallen trees that create rafts of floating weed are favoured. Safety from light, predators overhead and anglers are all important but I also think that some fish like to rub their flanks against underwater snags.

⅄ OPPORTUNISTS
Most fish species will take food wherever they can find it. Even fish that are predominantly bottom-feeders may well come to the surface to take a bait or natural foodstuffs, such as hatching flies. Lily beds are particularly attractive to surface feeders.

BECOMING FAMILIAR

To get the very best out of your fishing you need to pursue all the species with the whole variety of methods. However, it's a good idea to concentrate on one species at a time and only move on when you truly get to know a particular species' characteristics. Believe me, they're all different. For example, barbel and chub might inhabit the same river, but they feed very differently and often choose to live in different areas. Pike are particularly fascinating and, although you can pick up a general idea of how the species behaves, you will tend to find that behavioural patterns change from water to water and certainly from season to season.

Even within the same species, individuals can act very differently. For example, some fish will get caught over and over again. Some fish will be very much 'stay-at-home', whereas other characters will roam far and wide. Individual fish can even change their own longstanding habits, perhaps moving from their home of several years for no apparent reason.

Surprising Vulnerability

You'll often come across a big shoal of fish and you'll think the water is very prolific. This isn't necessarily the case. Fish aren't scattered randomly throughout the water like currants in a cake; they tend to congregate in specific, favoured areas. You might find one swim that's full of fish, but it's likely that there are many others completely devoid of life.

Furthermore, fish are invariably more fragile than you'd think. A pike might look indestructible with its big teeth and ferocious eyes, like something out of Jurassic Park, and indeed in the water it's a demon, a master hunter, but take it out of its environment and it becomes instantly vulnerable to bad handling. So, if we want our fishing to

⋏ THE CARING ANGLER
Michael holds this 28-pound pike very carefully: his hands support the frame of the fish, keeping clear of the sensitive organs in the stomach area, and his lap supports the gut.

⋎ A QUICK PHOTOGRAPH
If you are going to photograph your fish out of the water then do it as quickly as possible. These two fine barbel were held in the water until the photographer was ready to shoot.

continue well into the future we need to take the following thoughts on board. Firstly, fish populations are often nowhere near as dense as you might initially think and, secondly, individual fish must be treated with the utmost care and consideration. As a responsible angler, please, please remember these points each and every moment you're fishing.

Fish like to lead ordered lives based on long-established ground rules, and we, with our advanced tackle and bait, simply introduce troublesome elements into a balanced equation. Watch the fish – that's essential to good angling – but also watch out for the fish. Keep in mind that we are very much the guardians of the waterside. No one else in society is as intimately concerned with the welfare of fish as anglers are. We need fish in order to indulge our favourite sport, but we should also love fish because we understand them and appreciate their fascinating lifestyles and their exquisite physical beauty.

➤ GO WITH THE FLOW
A wondrous sunset, but this angler isn't admiring the scenery. Don't tie yourself to the bankside – if you think that a particular piece of water can be fished better from a mid-stream rock then make the effort to get as close to your fish as possible.

USING A THERMOMETER

Many anglers don't bother taking water temperatures when they go fishing because, they say, there's nothing they can do about what they'd find. All right, you can't make the water hotter or colder but the information the thermometer provides can be interesting and can be put to good use. For example, if the water is colder than you were expecting, it might pay you to target a different species, one that has greater tolerance of the cold.

It's also fascinating to check temperatures against feeding spells: if fish come on the feed suddenly and unexpectedly, your thermometer might tell you that it was a rise or fall in temperature of a crucial degree or two that provoked that feeding frenzy. Take water readings at different depths or under weed beds, for example. You might find quite wide ranges of temperature and realize one area of the water suits a particular fish species much more than the others.

A thermometer can help you detect the presence of an underwater spring, for example, that lowers the surrounding water temperature to a more acceptable level in the summer. Make a note, and go back the next time there's a heat wave.

WATERCRAFT

I BELIEVE THAT A GOOD ANGLER REALLY HAS TO UNDERSTAND WATER DEEPLY AND IN A THREE-DIMENSIONAL WAY. WATER IS A PHYSICAL SUBSTANCE, A VITAL ELEMENT TO THE FISH. THE LAKE, POND, RESERVOIR, STREAM OR RIVER IS THE FISH'S HOME. THE SUBTLE QUALITIES OF THE WATER BETWEEN THE BANKS DICTATES EXACTLY HOW AND WHERE THE FISH ARE GOING TO LIVE.

The nature of water has hugely important effects on your choice of tackle and bait. Given all the possibilities, there can seem a daunting amount to learn. You might well be an expert on one type of water and still be completely out of your depth in another. Never be intimidated: with thought, experience and patience, you can get to grips with any water type. A massive and terrifying unknown water soon becomes manageable once you've settled on a ground plan.

The Need for Observation

It is vital to remember that we are not fish and that we will never completely understand fish unless they learn to talk. It's all well and good looking at endless diagrams explaining where fish are likely to be found in any given lake or river. Many of them are accurate to a degree and promise some probability of success, but there are hundreds of cases where I've been completely fooled, where all my experience has been turned upside down. The perfect holding place for fish has proved to be absolutely barren, and the useless-looking place has been full of them. Logic has been defied over and over again, but this doesn't mean that fish do anything on a whim – there is a rationale behind every aspect of their behaviour.

The lesson is to keep an open mind and wide open eyes. Whether you're going to a new water or one you know well, take your time and don't be in too great a rush to start fishing. Indeed, if it's a new water you're visiting, I recommend leaving your tackle at home to avoid temptation, as a few hours spent walking and watching will pay vast dividends in the future, especially if you make the best use of your time.

◀ WELL HIDDEN
Never underestimate your quarry or take chances. Always keep low to the skyline, using whatever cover you can find to camouflage your movements, even if this means a certain amount of discomfort. The angler that puts in the real effort is the one that's going to be successful.

▶ INTO THE CAULDRON
What a place to fish! This really is extreme angling. Amazingly, fish can be landed from this terrifyingly steep ledge – provided you're prepared to scramble for quarter of a mile along the rocks and then get into a coracle to finish off the job!

OBSERVATION EQUIPMENT

1 HAT *A broad brim keeps the sun off your head and out of your eyes.*

2 BINOCULARS *These allow you to scan the water surface for signs of fish topping.*

3 BOOTS *Always choose a pair that are warm, well-fitting and waterproof.*

4 POLAROIDS *Reducing glare, these are your windows into the fish's world.*

5 BREAD *Many fish species adore the simple, ordinary shop-bought loaf.*

6 SKETCH PAD *A simple map can prove invaluable when planning your strategy.*

7 PEN AND THERMOMETER *These are essential aids, as the water temperature is an important piece of information.*

Seeing Beneath the Surface

You'll need equipment to help you unravel any water's mysteries. Polarizing sunglasses that actually take away the surface glare are the most essential aid any fisherman has ever been presented with, and it amazes me how many anglers don't even carry them. Not all glasses are equal, and this is one area where you tend to get what you pay for – more expensive glasses are likely to have better lenses and be more scratch-resistant. Think about the colour of the lenses, too: grey or dark shades are fine for very bright days, but slightly lighter lenses can maximize the light when the weather is dull. Above all, ask for good, reliable advice. Ask to borrow other anglers' glasses on the bankside: just half a minute wearing them will answer many questions. Also, make sure any polarizing glasses you buy fit snugly: if they're too tight you'll find them chafing on the nose or round the ears; too loose and, obviously, they'll be in eight feet of water before you can blink.

I hate wearing hats, personally, but there's no doubt that a big brim can cut down on the light entering your field of vision, so if you're going to wear a hat, a good brim is essential. Make sure it's light and cool for summer and warm and snug for winter, and if it's midge-proof so much the better. A sun flap at the back is also useful for hot climates.

We now come to one of the most overlooked of all anglers' aids: a pair of binoculars. Binoculars make time on the waterside much more enjoyable because you can watch the local wildlife, perhaps kingfishers, waterfowl and even a distant otter. So far so good, but what they really allow you to do is get up close and personal with the fish that you're watching. It's one thing to see a bass at a distance: put up your binoculars and you can actually see it feeding. Zoom in close and you'll even see what it's feeding on. What are those fish cruising round the island? Tench? Bream? Rudd? Dig out the binoculars and you'll get the answer.

Even when you're watching fish very close in, binoculars reveal much more about their lifestyle than you can ever pick up on with the naked eye. I have assumed that the carp that are lying motionless just beyond the rod tip are virtually dormant: look through the binoculars and you realize that's nonsense. In fact they're sucking in mouthfuls of water daphnia and earning themselves a

⌄ CAUGHT IN THE ACT!

If you are heron-like in your approach you'd be surprised just how close you can find the fish into the bank. This chub has come into water barely deep enough to cover its back to feed on samples of bait that have fallen from an angler's bucket. So, yes, you can catch fish in just six inches of water.

very good meal, and that's why they're oblivious to my baits!

A good, strong, preferably waterproof, notebook is also invaluable, the larger the better. You can draw profiles of swims. You can plot the patrol routes of bream shoals. You can record water levels, water visibility and water temperatures. Keep a record of any fish you might see in unusual places. Do this every time you visit a water. You'll soon begin to build up a set of notebooks on all the waters that you regularly fish and, gradually,

⌄ UP CLOSE AND PERSONAL

Binoculars truly are an invaluable aid. Not only do they let you appreciate wildlife on the riverbank, but they allow you to see precisely what fish are feeding on, how they are behaving and, sometimes, what's making them fearful.

you'll begin to appreciate trends that ordinary anglers just never pick up on at all. Your catch rates will obviously increase but, more importantly, you will also gain the satisfaction of being totally in tune with a favourite venue.

Keeping Comfortable

You'll be doing a lot of walking and watching, so make sure that your footwear is appropriate. Wellingtons are good, but waders or even chest waders are probably better – especially if you can afford Gore-Tex, which means that you keep cool on the hottest of days. It's often very useful indeed to get into shallow, safe water so that you can investigate food sources.

Make sure that your clothing is watertight and comfortable – cool for summer and warm for winter. Ensure that you've got something to sit upon. Take mosquito cream if necessary. Don't forget food and drink. If you're physically uncomfortable, you'll soon be making excuses to leave the water and get off home.

For this reason, choose carefully the days that you go water watching. It doesn't make sense to go in periods of wind, rain and cold: the water will be dour, visibility will be low, fish movement restricted and, in short, you're not going to learn much. Instead, choose calm, bright, warm weather – the water before you will be much more open and you'll find the fish active. If you can, get there early: the period just after dawn is frequently frantic. You'll learn a lot about fish movements, especially the areas they like to feed in. Equally, if you can stay until dusk then you'll get a second helping, although perhaps at a slightly lower level of intensity.

➢ CONCENTRATION
Notice the Polaroids – essential if you're going to watch the fish and what your bait is doing. The light chest waders are also vital if you're going to wade and walk in the heat of a summer's day. All your tackle can be fitted into the pockets of a jacket and the bait into a bucket slung on a belt (see picture opposite). Now you should feel free to roam, explore and really attack the river.

Structures and Features

So what are you actually looking for? Let's start by considering the most obvious bankside features and think carefully why they are attractive. For example, look out for a cattle drink on either a river or a lake. Chances are the animals will come to it a few times during the day, especially in hot weather. In a river, their activities will send a cloud of mud downstream. Fish learn to look within this cloud for dislodged organisms, and the muddied water hides your tackle. The same applies in a lake: once the cattle have departed, carp are often quick to come in to sift among the disturbed mud looking for bloodworm and tiny

insects. A cattle drink might initially look like a muddied up hole, but it can have its uses.

Watch the natural contour of the bank, especially where it steepens and enters the water at an angle: chances are that you'll have deep water close inshore at such places. It goes without saying that overhanging trees and bushes, especially if they're alive, provide both shelter and food. Look for areas of bank that are all but impenetrable: it is likely these zones get very little fishing pressure and wily fish are likely to be holed up here. Marginal weed beds are also very important for the same sort of reasons, as well

⋏ AROUND THE PILINGS

Get beneath the surface of a fast-flowing river and you'd be amazed at how the current pushes and pulls and how the weed sweeps backwards and forwards in an ever-moving carpet. There's also constant clutter in the flow: dead vegetation, scraps of rubbish and, of course, food items dislodged from the bottom.

as the fact that they frequently harbour huge amounts of food. Consider carefully how you can get a bait into these kinds of areas without causing damage – don't cut your way into a dense bed of bulrushes, for example, as you might disrupt nesting song birds.

Think carefully about manmade structures along the bank – dams, boathouses, jetties and quays and, of course, bridges. No angler can ever cross a bridge without looking over, and for good reason. Bridge pools are frequently the most attractive along any beat. The bridge supports deflect the current, and the pools created are often deep, dark and full of both food and fish. Bridges are great vantage points, and it always helps if you can actually look down on the fish that you're watching. Similarly, if you can establish climbing trees round a lake or along a riverbank you'll find them of great benefit – provided, of course, they're safe and that you're comfortable with heights.

On a river, look carefully at the current. Look for areas where it quickens or slows or changes direction. Look for eddies, calm areas off the main current. Note where the water boils like a cauldron. This indicates that the river is pushing over big obstacles down on the bottom, most commonly rocks, and these obstacles could attract fish in low water conditions, although the

water is likely to be too turbulent at flood time.

There are also innumerable water features that you ought to be looking out for from the bank. Islands are obvious and so, too, are the myriads of different water weed types – wherever there is weed there will be shade, protection, food and fish. With polarizing glasses you'll

⋏ VARIETY IS THE SPICE
A little weir like this can be invaluable in a hot summer when oxygen levels are low. Just a hint of white water will breathe new life into a stale stream and attract many fish.

⋎ THE TAIL OF THE GLIDE
This barbel swim is full of all manner of fish species. Why? Well, they all love the tail of a glide where the water shallows and speeds up and channels food towards them.

◄ WINTER CAMOUFLAGE
Get to know how your fish live. These perch have snuggled into dead foliage as the water temperatures plummet and thin ice forms above them. They probably won't feed again until warm winds come in bringing rain and rapidly climbing temperatures. They can feel secure, however, from predatorial attack: just look at how invisible their camouflage makes them.

THE VIEWING BANK
A high bank giving an unrestricted view of the water is always a bonus. Take time to sit there with binoculars watching the fish rolling, bubbling or simply cruising.

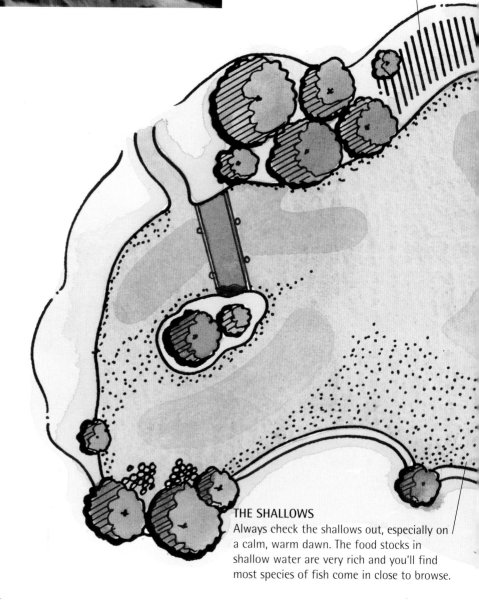

WATER FEATURES

• **Dam Walls** Dams are nearly always the deepest part of any still water. Check them out, especially in the hottest or coldest of weathers.

• **Old stream beds** Many lakes are built around old streams. Find the former course and you'll almost certainly discover deeper water.

• **Lilies** Fish love the shade of the pads and the food on the stems.

• **Reed beds** Fish investigate extensive reed beds for the rich supply of food.

• **Manmade structures** Check out boat sheds, jetties, old fishing platforms, sunken boats or jettisoned rubbish.

• **Islands** Fish will pack close to islands – especially in fresh waters.

• **Underwater springs** Many lakes are fed by underwater springs, which are a source of cool water in the summer and warmer water in the winter, hence they are always attractive areas for fish. Watch for springs as they plume on the surface.

THE SHALLOWS
Always check the shallows out, especially on a calm, warm dawn. The food stocks in shallow water are very rich and you'll find most species of fish come in close to browse.

actually be able to see into the water and make a note of all the features that attract fish – sunken branches and trees, rocks and boulders, overhangs, undercuts, drop-offs, ledges and even human cast-offs, from a shopping trolley to a dumped car! Watch for feeder streams or areas where fish-eating waterfowl are diving on a regular basis. Grebes, for example, perfectly signpost the shoals of small fish that bigger predators feed upon.

Try to visit all waters when the levels are down: you'll get a much clearer indication of what the bed is like and what features are present. Remember to put all this knowledge down in your notepad. You will see how much information there is, how it builds up and how it would be so easy to forget a vital brick in the wall.

THE WINDWARD SHORE

The predominant winds that hit this lake come from the west and the south. This means that they push, generally, towards the north-eastern tip of the lake. This is where the currents are at their strongest, pushing food here and there and often colouring the water. Accumulations of fish build up here, feeding hard... and the big predators know also just where they themselves are going to find a meal. Fishing into the wind can be a cold, painful process but you can see why it pays off.

THE DROP-OFF

Try to pinpoint any dramatic change in underwater topography. The ledge from shallow to deep water is particularly important and fish will follow it in their search for food.

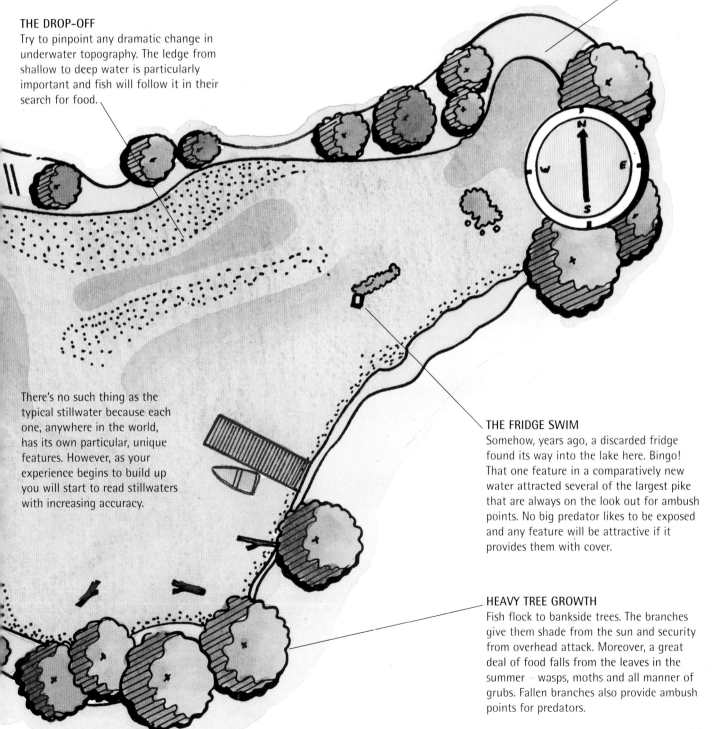

There's no such thing as the typical stillwater because each one, anywhere in the world, has its own particular, unique features. However, as your experience begins to build up you will start to read stillwaters with increasing accuracy.

THE FRIDGE SWIM

Somehow, years ago, a discarded fridge found its way into the lake here. Bingo! That one feature in a comparatively new water attracted several of the largest pike that are always on the look out for ambush points. No big predator likes to be exposed and any feature will be attractive if it provides them with cover.

HEAVY TREE GROWTH

Fish flock to bankside trees. The branches give them shade from the sun and security from overhead attack. Moreover, a great deal of food falls from the leaves in the summer – wasps, moths and all manner of grubs. Fallen branches also provide ambush points for predators.

Looking for Signs

You're not here to look simply at the water but also at the fish. You've got to learn to recognize not just the fish themselves but also the signs that they give off. For example, many kinds of fish send up bubbles when they feed. The water might be too deep to see the type of fish involved but the bubbles themselves give a clue. For example, tench bubbles tend to be small, numerous and tightly clustered. Carp bubbles tend to be larger and follow a mazy trail as the carp meanders along its feeding bed. In rivers, barbel also send up bubbles, often accompanied by a stain of brown water as they clear away the silt. Binoculars and sunglasses once again help a great deal in spotting the bubbles and sometimes in identifying the culprits.

There are a host of other signs that indicate what species of fish you're looking at; look out for fin shapes – tench have more rounded fins, whereas those of bream are more angular. Look for the long dorsal fin of a carp to differentiate it from a bream or, in rivers, a barbel or chub. Look for the black tail fin that signifies a large-mouth bass. When watching predators, be aware that a pike likes to take its prey with a single, violent thrust, whereas perch will often pursue the prey fish over several yards, harrying it, attacking its tail, slowing it down before a catch is made. Also, if several attacks are made at once into a group of shoal fish then the chances are that perch, zander or even bass are the marauders, rather than the more solitary pike.

Look also for signs of earlier fish activity: if the lake or riverbed has even the finest covering of silt, feeding areas are not hard to find as they will be polished clear and stand out distinctly in good light and clear

water. Sometimes the feeding is so violent that a slight depression is also created. If you are on the water for some time, it often pays to introduce bait into areas where it can be seen clearly on the bottom: go back to check it at various times throughout the day to see if it's gone or if there are fish feeding upon it. You don't get much clearer clues than these to the whereabouts of feeding fish and the bait to use.

⋏ BUBBLES!
Learn to read your bubbles. You can often tell the species that is making them and by watching their direction closely you can plot exactly where to place a bait. Natural baits are excellent for bubbling fish because, of course, that's what they're feeding on.

⋎ SPAWNING FRENZY
Visit your local waters during spawning time and you'll be able to get within touching distance of the fish. This will give you a really strong impression of the fish stocks of the lake and their maximum sizes.

PLUMBING THE DEPTHS

On a new water, always take time out to investigate swims as thoroughly as possible and log your discoveries. A knowledge of the varying depths is basic to your understanding, and this can be gained by plumbing the swims. The basic tackle is shown in the diagram and consists of a two-ounce weight, a couple of beads and a marker float – a big pike float will do for this job. It's the simplest of rigs and the simplest of methods. Cast out, wind down until the float is tight against the lead and then, once you know the float is at the bottom, you can pay off line a foot at a time until it reappears. By counting the length of line off carefully you will find the exact depth of the swim in different places. Sketch a quick map of the swim and mark the depths down in a notebook so you don't forget them.

You can also pick up other clues at the same time. For example, if your lead comes back covered in weed, you'll have some idea of the nature and amount of weed that's out there. When you're dragging the lead around, if it feels free then in all probability you are sliding it back through silt and soft mud. If you feel sharp taps and raps then chances are it's gravel and small stones. Heavy pressure followed by slackening indicates that you've pulled the lead over a gravel bar. Weed is a sullen, almost dead, resistance.

⋏ THE GEAR
Plumbing gear is quite simple: a large marker float, a two-ounce bomb and two large rubber shot beads on the line complete the rig.

⋏ LET OUT AND RELINE
Let line off the reel in carefully measured distances and the float will not only rise to the surface but it will also provide a record of the depth of the water at that point.

IMPORTANT CONTOURS
Even the smallest of ponds will nearly always have features that aren't visible from the surface but that dictate how the fish behave and where they travel and feed. On many large waters there are mazes of gravel bars, channels and plateaux. Time taken to build up an accurate plan is never wasted.

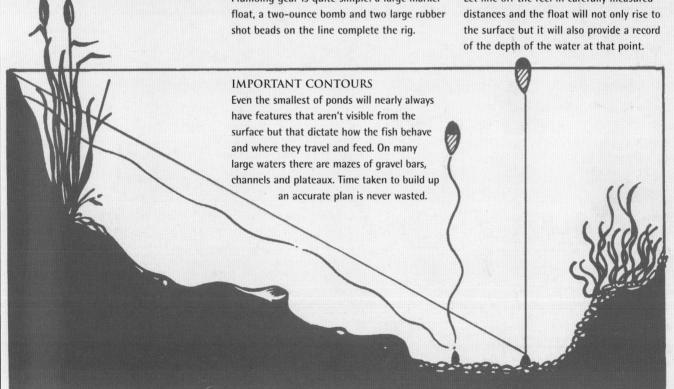

GETTING AFLOAT

There are many benefits to physically getting out on the water you want to fish. You can easily plumb depths. You can see where the weed beds are and spot any potential snags. You'll often see fish. You'll be able to see whether ground bait has been eaten. You will even be able to retrieve lost gear. However, there are some important dos and don'ts.

• Always check the fishery rules and ensure that you're not annoying fellow anglers.
• Don't go out unless you're a strong swimmer, and always wear a buoyancy aid.
• Never go out in rough weather or when rough weather is expected.
• It's best to have a friend on the bank and if you're at all unsure then link yourself to him or her with a long, thin rope.
• The float tube has conquered the fly-fishing world but has been surprisingly slow to make inroads into bait fishing. You simply pump it up, fit yourself into it and paddle yourself away. They are relatively cheap, safe and very manoeuvrable. You can probably get closer to fish in a float tube than any other way.
• A wide, stable canoe is an ideal vessel to get you around any waterway. The problem is getting it to the water – you'll need a roof rack or a trailer.

⋏ WHERE OTHERS FEAR TO TREAD

There are times when a canoe or boat offer the only way of getting into impenetrable areas, especially on large or overgrown waters. Canoes are particularly useful as they can often be easily transported on a car roof rack, for example.

• Inflatable boats can be excellent. They pack down small and are easily inflated using a modern pump that runs from the car cigarette lighter socket. Inflatables are easily paddled and highly manoeuvrable.

Keep On Watching

Even when you are actually fishing, providing your tackle is safe, don't hesitate to take time out, pick up your glasses and binoculars and go for a good, long stroll along the bank. Not only are you likely to come across feeding fish in different areas but you'll also be resting your own swim, which can be very beneficial. The longer your tackle is in any particular swim, the more stressed and wary the fish are likely to become. Give the swim a rest and you'll probably find it much easier to get a bite on your return.

⋏ KEEP MOVING

The more swims you fish, the more you build up an overall picture of the river. It's also much kinder to the fish stocks to catch one or two specimens and then move on to the next shoal.

➤ OVER EXPOSED

It's very difficult to fish a barren piece of water like this truly effectively, but the angler would have been better off fishing either sitting down or from a kneeling position. It's often a good idea to cast your bait out and then gently move back up the bank, often ten yards or more, so that you're well sheltered.

The important thing is always to feel at ease with the water you're fishing and to feel that your knowledge is steadily building up. Don't ever feel over-awed: if you are looking at a huge water, maybe several miles in length, then separate it into distinct zones: decide to examine a bay, for example, or an area close to a dam or an inflowing stream or river. Look carefully at each particular part of the water and your overall impression of it will slowly build into a solid picture.

TACKLE

Tackle is important – it is the tool of your trade. Choose your tackle with care, look after it and make sure it's always in tiptop condition. If you let your tackle down then, chances are, it's going to disappoint you and often at a critical moment. Every week there are new developments in tackle – keep your eye on these so you're not left behind.

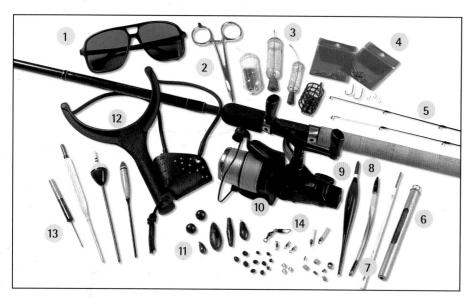

STANDARD FISHING TACKLE

1 POLAROID GLASSES *Allow you to see beneath the surface glare.*

2 FORCEPS *For easy hook removal and flattening hook barbs.*

3 SWIM FEEDERS *A selection will suit different waters and conditions.*

4 HOOKS *Always take a selection of hook sizes for different types of bait.*

5 QUIVER TIPS *These offer good bite indication.*

6 THERMOMETER *It's always useful to know the water temperature, and many experts take a thermometer.*

7 WAGGLER FLOAT *A transparent waggler float for still or slow waters.*

8 QUILL FLOAT *Perfect for close-in lake fishing.*

9 AVON TYPE FLOAT *For fast water and big baits.*

10 FIXED SPOOL REEL *The best of buys.*

11 LEGER WEIGHTS *A selection, including bombs and bullets.*

12 BAIT CATAPULT *Allows you to fire small bait (e.g. maggots) far from the bank.*

13 RIVER FLOATS *A selection, together with a baiting needle.*

14 TERMINAL TACKLE *Shot to weight, swivels to prevent the line twisting, beads and float rubbers are all part of the kit.*

Detailed lists of the tackle you may need for specific situations will be given in each of the chapters in the second part of this book, when we look at particular fish species and waters. Here, I just want to put the focus on tackle in a more generalized, thoughtful fashion.

I think it's important to get certain basics across without over-complicating a simple issue. After all, tackle is designed purely to put out a bait, register a bite, play a fish and land it. You will come across lots of tackle buffs in the fishing world and peace be with them if that's their over-riding passion. Don't be deluded though: simply choose tackle to do the job and then concentrate on the fish, the water, and the bait and method you're going to require. Don't be a slave to the latest fads and fancies. It really doesn't matter what colour your rod's whippings are providing it has the eyes in the right places.

➤ A LUCKY CAPTURE
This big barbel really had me beat and I was extraordinarily lucky to eventually pull it from some underwater snags. My end tackle was in shreds and you can see exactly what I mean by looking at the photograph on page 41... the hook was almost straightened and the line above it was frayed to the point of breaking.

The Right Rod for the Job

When you're choosing a rod, take your time. Don't be rushed. In my view, it's best not to buy mail order because you really need to hold the rod and test it out against others before making a decision. If possible, try to use a rod on the bankside before making a purchase. Perhaps a friend or fellow angler has the model that you're eyeing. Ask for all the advice you can and read what magazines make of the latest models. Trust your own judgement in the end, however, as you're the one who has to fish with

the rod in the years to come. You can rest assured that virtually all the rods made by the leading companies these days are excellent in both design and quality.

Make sure that you're absolutely clear in your mind what purpose you have in mind for your new rod. Sometimes a compromise is forced upon you, but don't sacrifice your initial ideas entirely. How does the rod feel in your hand? Does it balance nicely with your own reel? Don't just waggle the rod or let its tip be pulled down by the shop owner. Actually put the line through

▾ IMMENSE PRESSURE
This is when a through-action rod like this really comes into its own. Neils is trying to stop a 200-pound beluga sturgeon in its tracks and the rod is really taking the strain. If the action wasn't as complete as this and restricted to the top section only, a break would be almost inevitable. As it is, the rod bends right down to the handle and exerts immense power.

the rings and see how it copes then. What guarantee is being offered with the rod? Does it come with a travelling tube? Do you think you need one of the excellent four- or five-piece models now available that can be broken down and stowed away in an aircraft locker? This is a very important point for the travelling fisherman.

Always go to a tackle shop that has plenty of choice, and don't be afraid to compare as many rods as possible. Choose a tackle shop with a good reputation and that way you won't be palmed off with something the dealer's been looking to get rid of for years. It has often been said that choosing a rod is like looking for a partner – making a match that should last for life. I'll make no comment on that, but a good rod should become a firm and trusted friend for many years to come.

⋏ AT CLOSE QUARTERS
My great friend Johnny Jensen is closing in on a small but spirited taimen taken on a lure. Notice how Johnny's left hand is positioned well up the rod round the first rod ring. This gives him greater leverage over the fish and he can power it towards him. Keep your rod well up at this point to absorb the plunges of the fish, and set the reel's clutch loose enough to give line to the final runs of the fish.

Choosing a Reel

When it comes to the reel even simpler qualifications apply. You simply want one that holds enough line of the diameter you need, casts without fuss and plays a fish well, probably through its slipping clutch. Rugged reliability is also an important consideration. Size, therefore, is important. There's no point tackling large, pit carp with a tiny reel only capable of holding 50 or 60 yards of line.

Match the reel to the job. Make sure the reel feels nice, is well finished and that there is no undue vibration when you turn the handle. Test the clutch carefully: modern clutches should be super-smooth with no need for a sharp pull to set them into motion.

The important criteria are reliability, spool size, casting ability and the slipping clutch.

The Centre Pin

Let's think about other reel aspects. Most reels are of a standard fixed-spool design and these work well for virtually all bait-fishing situations. However, if you are doing much river fishing then an English-style centre pin is a tremendous tool to own. It really does allow you to trot a float or big bait down with the current under perfect control. Even an excellent caster won't be able to put tackle out huge distances with a centre pin, but for close-in river work it's hard to beat. Many anglers also like a centre pin for marginal work when fishing for carp on lakes. Playing a fish on a centre pin is dynamic: there are no gears between you and the power of the fish, and that really transmits itself up through the rod.

⋏ THE CENTRE PIN
The centre pin is the craftsman's reel and it's most at home on river work; the ideal weapon for trotting a float. Playing a fish on a centre pin is also a joy – there are no gears to dull the sensation and it's a raw, direct experience.

⋎ THE FIXED SPOOL REEL
This is the world's favourite. Beautifully engineered, light and easy to use it can cast over 100 yards and has the power to play a 100-pound fish! This is the reel for 80 per cent of all fishing situations.

⋏ RIVER JOY
A fine barbel and the centre pin reel and trotting float that helped accomplish its downfall. There is an art to fishing and the river float fisherman knows this only too well.

The Multiplier

For really heavy work a multiplier reel is the tool you'll need. Perhaps you're trolling for pike on vast waters or fishing for mahseer in India. These are situations where the reel will be subjected to immense pressures and must hold vast lengths of high-diameter line – which is where the multiplier comes into its own.

Then we have the lightweight multipliers, the bait caster reels designed to flick plugs, spinners, spoons and rubber jigs with highly focused accuracy. These are the tools for the bass fisherman and general predator angler. They are light, they are reliable and they give you infinite control. They might not be quite as easy to use as the fixed-spool reel initially, but once you've got the hang of it there's nothing to beat them for the job.

⋏ PRACTICE IS THE KEY
Take time to practise with your multiplier before finding yourself actually fishing with it. Go to a local playing field and check out the casting. You need to develop a smooth, pendulum-type action and learn to slow the spool with your thumb just before the lead touches down to avoid over-runs and bird nests. Timing is critical, but practice makes perfect.

Hooks and the Rest

These days there is a bewildering variety of hooks on display at any good tackle shop. Once again, ask advice and make sure the hooks that you choose are exactly suited for the purpose in mind. Never go out without a wide variety of hook sizes: you don't know if the successful bait on the day is going to be a fraction of worm or a great hunk of bread flake, and it's stupid to be caught out. There are all manner of different hook designs on the market, but the over-riding concerns are strength and sharpness. Don't pursue any fish in a situation where the hook you're using could bend and straighten. As for sharpness, many hooks these days are chemically etched and keep a point well. Filing these is of no particular benefit, but do check standard hooks for sharpness: one method is just to run the point over your nail to see if it makes a slight impression.

A big issue is whether to go barbless: there's little real doubt that a barbless hook is best for the fish, so

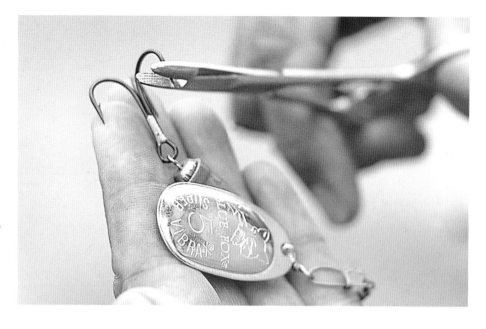

I'd recommend it. Alternatively, go for a micro-barbed hook or simply flatten the barb down on a normal hook with a pair of forceps. Barbless hooks also have the advantage of slipping out of human flesh much more easily!

When it comes to leads and feeders, think carefully about what a swim needs and what your best approach will be. Sound travels extraordinarily clearly through

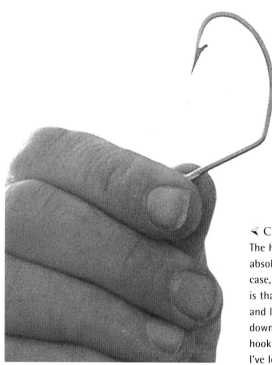

◄ CHOOSE WITH CARE
The hook I'm holding here has been absolutely mashed by a large fish – in this case, a giant catfish. The only good thing is that I didn't actually have a breakage and leave the hook in the fish. The fault is down to me: I really should have chosen a hook with stronger wire, but it's a lesson I've learnt well.

⊼ TREBLE DANGER
Treble hooks always cause more harm to a fish than a single, so make sure that their damage potential is limited to the full. The best way is to either use barbless trebles or squash the barbs down with forceps. Use the smallest trebles that you can get away with, as bigger ones simply inflict more damage.

water, and a heavy lead or heavy feeder will be heard and felt by fish many yards away. For this reason, don't use more weight on your line than you actually need. Think, too, about what the fish see: a bright silver lead flashes in the sunlight and really advertises itself, and so do some of the garish feeder colours. My advice as a diver is to go for subtle leads and feeders that merge into the background as much as possible.

The same advice goes for float choice: don't use such a light float that you can't control your tackle, but bear in mind that a heavier float automatically creates more disturbance. Think, too, about the size of your float: in shallow, clear water you don't want too much float under the surface, especially if the fish are wary, and it's a mistake to delude yourself that a transparent plastic float won't be seen: it will.

◄ A CLOSE SHAVE
You've already seen the fish that inflicted this damage and read the story (see page 34). Quite obviously the hook just wasn't up to the job and, considering the swim, I should have gone for a heavier pattern. The line, too, only just held on. It was one of the new co-polymer lines, which are extraordinarily strong for their diameter but do wear quite quickly. A standard monofilament would probably have done the job better. Look at the other major risk I took. Notice how the split shot is simply pinched onto the line. This, again, can cause a severe weakening. To avoid this, put a thin rubber sleeve on the line and attach the shot to this sleeve so that the nylon itself isn't gripped.

The Line

Over the last few years there have been huge advances in the design of lines. In general, diameters have come down and strength has gone up. However, do be aware of a few considerations. A lot of the ultra-thin lines are of co-polymer construction. This gives amazing strength-to-diameter possibilities, but many co-polymer lines are susceptible to abrasion and can break unexpectedly. This goes for a lot of modern lines that concentrate exclusively on strength. If you are fishing a rocky or snaggy area then it pays to look for a brand that advertises its resistance to abrasion.

Think carefully whether you are going to use braid or monofilament. Braid has many advantages: it's very limp and it's easy to cast and it's also very fine for its incredible strength. For these reasons, many fishermen – lure anglers especially – like to use

braid, but be warned. Like co-polymer line, braid can snap very quickly and most unexpectedly in some rocky situations.

Today, lines come in a bewildering array of different colours, so where on earth do you begin? Well, there's a general feeling that the more closely the line merges in with the overall water colour the better. After years of diving, I'm not absolutely sure this is the case, but it never pays to take chances and you might as well cover all possible options.

Never be tempted to use too fine a line for the situation in the hope that you'll buy more bites that way. What's the point of getting more bites if you simply lose the fish? Check your line carefully after any gruelling battle – especially the last few yards, which take a lot of the strain. If you're in any doubt whatsoever, take the line off and re-spool. You should take great care of your line, storing it away from sunlight and also ensuring that all knots are really secure.

➤ KEEPING UP THE PRESSURE
If you've got confidence in your gear then you'll play a fish at maximum power. This keeps the fight short, which is good for both your nerves and the fish. Don't let the fish dictate. Here, Alan, with watchful guide Anthony, plays his fish with real bravado and it works. A big multiplier reel was the perfect tool to land the large catfish that was soon to emerge.

Quality Accessories

These are by far your major items although, of course, tackle shops are full of goodies that might or might not be necessary. As a general rule, always buy the best that you can afford on the assumption that the quality will be high: for example, you don't want a landing net with a handle that breaks!

Clothing is very important, so don't skimp here. If you're cold in the winter then your concentration will suffer and you will find yourself packing in, probably just before the fish start to feed. Warm clothing is so advanced these days there is simply no excuse to be cold, even in temperatures of -30°C.

High-quality luggage is also important: there's nothing more frustrating than having a tackle bag break on you, especially if you're walking long distances.

∀ BLENDING IN
If you're going to adopt a more static approach to your fishing, then think carefully how you can make yourself as inconspicuous as possible. Trees and heavy reed growth all mask an angler and his tackle.

Keep a very close eye indeed upon tackle developments, and this means reading magazines carefully or paying regular visits to your tackle shop. Look at what is new and analyze whether it is useful for you. We're never going to re-invent the rod or the reel, but there are all sorts of creations that come onto the market every year that make life just that little bit simpler. Don't be dismissive of new developments, but don't be overly starry-eyed either. Get all the information, try it out for yourself if you think it might be

⋏ THE RIVER ANGLER
The photograph says it all – a glimpse of a centre pin reel, sweetcorn bait and a couple of quivers full of trotting floats. Float choice is critical. Don't choose a float that's too light or you won't have sufficient control. Think about the colour, too, because visibility is a keen point. A last tip: don't over-fill a centre pin spool, because under pressure the line can bed in and make casting difficult; 60 or 70 yards is generally quite sufficient.

worthwhile, and make your own assessment.

Your tackle is a major investment, so look after it. Keep it away from the damp and away from rod-handle nibbling rodents! Don't forget that unused bait in the garden shed is a particular attraction for animals. It's also wise to have your tackle insured with a policy that covers the tackle at home, in transit and on the waterside itself. Replacement can be expensive, as well as stressful.

➤ CASPIAN SEA MONSTER
What a sight! A Beluga sturgeon up from the Caspian Sea is nearing the boat. This fish is getting on for 200 pounds in weight and it needs super gear to land it. Notice again the multiplier reel and the uptide boat rod that is generally used in sea fishing. This is what we call a real 'through-action' and it bends right down to the butt to take the strain of a huge fish in fast water. The line was 50-pound breaking strain with a 100-pound leader; bait was half a dead fish.

BAIT

THERE IS NO SUCH THING AS THE ULTIMATE KILLER BAIT FOR EVERY
SPECIES IN EVERY SITUATION… FORTUNATELY. JUST IMAGINE HOW
DRAB FISHING WOULD BE IF SUCCESS WERE GUARANTEED. IT'S ALSO
WRONG TO PUT UNDUE FAITH IN ANY SINGLE BAIT, EVEN THOUGH
WE ALL HAVE OUR FAVOURITES. FISH WISE UP TO BAITS AND TURN
OFF THEM AFTER THEY'VE BEEN CAUGHT UPON THEM.

Most decades see a new wonder bait: once it was sweetcorn, then it was boilies, followed by special pastes and pellets. Considering the inventiveness of the human mind and the commercial drive of the angling industry, we can be pretty sure there will be new wonder baits out in the future: by all means test them out. Adopt them wherever necessary but don't discard the old. Let me give one typical example:

silkweed! Silkweed is simply the filamentous weed that grows in the swift water around weirs. It used to be a favourite in England among Victorian and Edwardian anglers a century ago but has long since fallen out of use. However, on a recent trip to Spain, we found that the only bait big barbel would look at was clumps of silkweed! It was like turning the clock back. We modern anglers who thought we knew everything were utterly dumbfounded. What anglers

of a hundred years ago would have started out with took us two full days to stumble upon. Watch out for the arrogance of modernity when it comes to your angling ideas!

➤ OLD TUNNEL MOUTH
Nick is cradling a 70-pound mahseer in southern India. Just look at that mouth! It's almost wide enough to fit Nick's head in. Remember that many fish can extend their mouths to tunnel-like extremities and sometimes a huge bait can make a really big and instant impact.

BAIT SELECTION

1. **BREAD** *Use your loaf… sliced bread is a perfect hookbait.*

2. **SAUSAGE** *Cooked sausage can be cut into slices.*

3. **LUNCHEON MEAT** *This can be cut into any shape and stays on the hook well.*

4. **CHEESE SPREAD** *Creates an excellent bait when mixed into a paste with bread.*

5. **CRUSTS** *Chunks of floating crust are especially good for carp.*

6. **SWEETCORN** *is an effective bait for most non-predatory fish species.*

7. **FRUIT** *Even the humble banana will attract fish such as chub.*

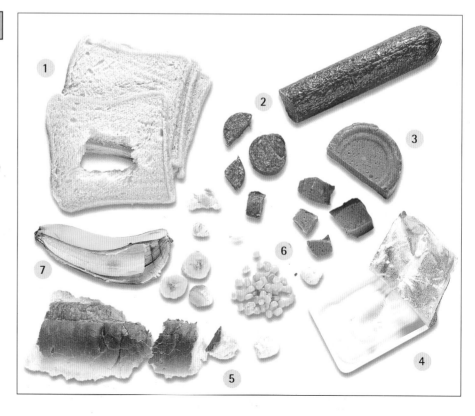

Timeless Favourites

This brings me neatly to traditional baits. Just because a bait hasn't been used for years doesn't mean that it is old-fashioned or useless. Fish, like humans, don't change their tastes over night. Bread, for example, is as old a bait form as there is. It can be used in crust, flake or paste form and it works. Virtually all fish have come across bread in one shape or another during the course of their natural lives. They both like and recognize the taste and smell. Bread is also easily seen both in coloured water and at night. You can use bread big or small, floating or sinking, and be confident that most fish swimming, bar the predators, will revel in it.

Cheese has many of the same qualities and, moreover, there is an

⋏ OFF THE TOP

Carp are renowned surface feeders, but don't overlook floating baits for other species. If there is a problem with surface fishing, it's the line. It stands out like a rope if there's nothing around it to break up the profile. Look for lily pads or weed beds to mask the telltale line.

⋖ ⋏ END RIGS

Never use a heavier weight than is strictly necessary, simply because the splash alerts fish instantly to your cast. Remember that sound travels five times further under water than it does in the air. Experiment with different hook lengths. Sometimes short is good but at other times a hook length of two yards is necessary for cautious, slow-biting fish.

◀ GROUND BAITING

In many circumstances ground baiting is an effective technique. Use imagination: use the juices of sweetcorn and the oils from hemp seed to flavour the ground bait base. Mix in attractive particle foodstuffs, such as casters. Remember that grains of rice keep fish rooting for hours because they're so small and plentiful.

▼ BREAD FLAKE

This is one of the most successful and adaptable baits for many species. Fresh, white, sliced bread is best. Tear a good chunk from the middle of a slice, push the hook through and squeeze the bread round the shank, leaving the hook point free.

endless variety to try out. Virtually all fish adore cheese either on its own or made into a paste with bread, but it's a sadly overlooked bait. How many barbel anglers, for example, do you see using cheese today, and yet it was an absolute favourite just a few years ago. You can go up market with the latest soft French cheeses or simply opt for the age-old cheese slices that might not be the gourmet's favourite but certainly work with chub, roach, barbel and carp.

Let's not forget luncheon meat, which really burst upon the scene in the 1960s. Most anglers cut it into cubes that can be coloured and scented if necessary. Alternatively, make it into a real rubby-dubby, mixed up with all manner of juices from corn, maggots and hemp. Be wary of cheap luncheon meat, as it's often very soft and difficult to cast. Go for more expensive brands with a higher percentage of meat. Buy a few cans and test them out for yourself: those with a strong, smoky taste often work well.

Particle Baits

Particle baits were all the rage before they even assumed the name! Particle baits are simply small baits used in large quantities, and they often attract the full attention of feeding fish. The original and most used particle bait of all is, obviously, the maggot or its chrysalis form, the caster. There are endless types of maggot according to the fly type originally used. Virtually every tackle shop sells them, often dyed in a multitude of colours, and maggots work. Whether it is one on a tiny hook or a bunch on a large hook, many fish species find them irresistible, especially when they've been fed into the swim in large quantities. Fish that do become wise to maggots will frequently switch over to casters, liking the colour and that crunch as they chew.

Another old favourite particle bait is hemp. Many species of fish become totally focused on the small black seeds, which, once stewed, open up to offer tantalizing glimpses of white and an irresistible smell in the water.

▼ UNDERWATER WORK

I learnt to dive some eight or nine years ago and you learn many things if you spend time diving with the fish you hope to catch. First of all you appreciate their grace underwater. You also begin to appreciate just how clumsy our attempts at catching them are. In bright, clear conditions for example, line often stands out like a dagger, glinting back the sun's rays. You realize that fish can see floats and leads – why not try using a stone superglued to a snap link instead? Sound, too, is very important and every footfall on the bankside above sounds like thunder beneath the surface. The lessons are obvious: take your time to work out a strategy; make that first cast as effectively as possible; try to mask your tackle among reeds or weeds.

There are several problems with particle baits: firstly, the fish become so preoccupied with them they often won't look at larger hook baits used over a bed of these particles. You've therefore got to use the particles on the hook and presentation can be difficult. Also, especially in summer, fry and fingerlings can be a problem when using maggots, not to mention the eels that sneak out as the dusk falls! So, while particles can turn your swim into a foaming pile of bubbles, they can also make a rod for your own back.

That's where slightly larger particles, such as sweetcorn, scored from the 1970s onward. Sweetcorn is easy to come by, no problem to prepare, easy to present and the fish turn onto it quickly. Sadly, fish also wise up quickly, too: the colour and the scent are probably just so distinctive that fish can soon learn to associate them with danger. Dying the grains black or, especially, red can prolong the life of the bait.

As sweetcorn exploded onto the scene and then began to fade, other seeds, legumes and nuts began to prove successful – peanuts (properly prepared), tiger nuts, tares, butter beans, brazil nuts, broad beans, cashew nuts, kidney beans, soy beans, chick peas, black-eyed beans… the list is quite endless. A few anglers have even used jelly babies with success! All these baits work well, probably for comparatively short periods, but they are so numerous that you can keep chopping and changing and coming up with a winning formula. Having said all this, however, it remains a fact that many highly successful anglers simply make do with bread, sweetcorn, maggots and casters throughout their careers.

⅋ END TACKLE

Think carefully about the business end of your tackle, what the fish actually sees. What size, shape and colour will suit any particular swim best? Will a flat lead hold bottom better in a quick current? Keep things simple: the more swivels and links that you use the more likelihood there is of a tangle. Think hard about your hook length, too, and keep experimenting.

⅄ FROM THE KITCHEN

Baits don't necessarily have to be fancy and complicated to catch fish, and a quick stop at a supermarket can often produce all that you need for a session. Bread, cheese, sausage, sweetcorn, even strips of bacon or pieces of meat pie will do the trick in very many circumstances. These pump out an attractive mixture of smells and flavours under water.

Hi-Tech Options

A far cry from the natural is the laboratory-produced special bait, a boiled bait or a paste consisting of endless amounts of carefully prepared, chemical-based ingredients. The notorious boily has, in short, revolutionized fishing for big fish. It's an item that usually consists of a dried powder added to eggs and flavouring, mixed into a paste, rolled into balls, boiled to give it a hard skin and then fed into the water. This is a

⊰ POP UPS

This photograph was taken at six feet or so down in a clear carp lake. The boily is buoyant so that it can carry the weight of the hook and waver tantalizingly just off the bed. This both makes it highly visible to a cruising fish and also allows it to be sucked into the mouth with the minimum of effort.

Using Natural Baits

Natural baits will always catch fish simply because they are there in the wild forming a part of the everyday menu. Don't overlook worms, caddis grubs, shrimps, slugs, wasp grubs and bloodworms. I'd like to also list such things as swan mussels and crayfish, but nowadays pollution, disease and a downturn in water quality has meant that some of these delicate, aquatic creatures are in short supply.

You can buy worms commercially or pick them from the surface of any grassland on a warmish, moist night. Look after your worms, keep them damp and throw away any dead or dying ones that will infect the healthy. In fact, if I had to restrict myself to just one bait for ever more, then my choice would probably be lobworms. They are immensely adaptable. They can be chopped up to form a really enticing ground bait or used singly or in bunches to attract any fish species from roach to salmon. Moreover, they are exactly what river fish expect to find after heavy rain.

➢ WRIGGLERS

Thousands of worms are washed to their death during floods along river systems each year and fish have come to recognize them as a safe, nutritious food. Caddis grubs are another great natural bait. They inhabit the bottom of the river living in cases glued to stones and gravel. Prise them out of their stony little cocoon to gain yourself one of the most unsuspected of all baits.

➢ CREEPY-CRAWLIES

Slugs are a good bait for many fish, especially chub. The size of hook depends on the type of slug used. Try, if you can, to use a slug without any weight on at all – they're often heavy enough to counteract a slight current. Look out also for all manner of nymphs, leeches, crickets, grasshoppers, moths, snails... anything of hookable size that is on the natural menu.

➢ DEAD BAITS

Nearly all fish species, not just the obvious predators, are fish eaters at sometime or another. Carp and even bream can be picked up on small dead fish from time to time. Chub and barbel adore them. Minnows like this can easily be caught in a lemonade bottle with a hole punctured at the bottom and a little bread bait sprinkled inside.

very simple description of a most complex system of baits. Most of them are based on high-protein mixes with all manner of essences and additives to make them taste, smell and look good. Boilies can be made buoyant to 'pop up' from the bottom so that they hang enticingly above weed or silt. Mini-boilies are also on the market – perfect for barbel, chub and roach. You can make your boilies – a time-consuming and rather messy, smelly business – or you can buy them, and there is a vast number of different varieties on offer.

The same goes for pastes and pellets, both of which have experienced a boom in recent years. Like boilies, paste and pellets can be bought from the local tackle shop and are easy to prepare and use. They have a great smell and this makes them particularly effective in low visibility waters where the fish don't hunt by sight.

⚹ CAREFUL PREPARATION
It's always a good idea to be prepared. These floating dog biscuits have had a groove filed along their underside. This fits the hook shank neatly and then the biscuit is superglued into position. This way you know the biscuit won't come off for at least an hour or so in the water.

⚹ BREAKDOWN
Think carefully about how your bait and the free offerings around it behave in the water. Pellets, for example, gradually break down, especially in warm water. What you get then are piles of enticing, powdery food that the fish love to hoover up.

MAKING BOILIES

I don't propose to go through the entire process of making boilies here, because the recipes can be picked up from the packets of the ingredients you will need to buy, but I will pass on a number of useful tips.

• Before starting to make boilies, always wash your hands really carefully in unscented water.
• Make sure all the utensils that you use are really clean.
• If you're going to make boilies on a regular basis then it pays to invest in modern tools such as sausage guns and rolling tables.
• Never smoke when you're making bait.
• Always use boiling water at every stage of the game. Hot water isn't good enough.

• Always follow the instructions on the packets and don't cut corners.
• Ensure that you measure ingredients exactly and don't make haphazard guesses. You'll need proper measuring equipment for this.
• Don't exceed the recommended dosage – you'll kill the bait totally.
• Have everything in front of you before

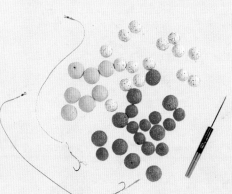

you begin. Baits will go off if you have to rush out for forgotten ingredients.
• Make sure everything you use is fresh – especially the eggs.
• Mix everything thoroughly.
• Tidy everything up and wash everything thoroughly once you've finished.
• Allow baits to cool and then store them carefully.
• Develop a smooth-running routine and you'll soon be turning baits out like a mini factory!

◁ DIY BOILIES
By making your own boilies you can come up with unique recipes, colours and even sizes. On hard-fished waters something that the carp have never seen before can very often give you the edge that you need. But don't go over the top – putting in too much flavour or colour, for example, can ruin a bait.

Baiting the Swim

What about ground bait? Well, you can ground bait with samples of your hook bait and this is often quite enough. There are times, however, when you want something a little more noticeable, and that's where a ground bait that explodes in the water, giving plenty of visual impact, comes into its own. The oldest and most commonly used form of ground bait is simply breadcrumb, but in the modern world the new ground baits have all manner of additives to increase their scent and visual attractiveness. Consistency is important, too: light ground bait can be used for shallow, still water, whereas heavier ground baits will be needed for quick, deep rivers. Choose with care, ask for advice, read the packet and, above all, ask yourself whether you need ground bait in the first instance. Always think carefully about any bait you're going to use and why. Try to get to a water beforehand and see what other anglers are using: sometimes it's wise to follow suit, but more often you should make up your own mind and go for something slightly different. Anglers who follow the crowd rarely lead it.

Luring the Predator

For the predator angler, bait really falls into two categories – natural or artificial. Certainly, if the water is

↖ BOMBARDMENT

Think about this shot carefully: the placing of the bait is good. It's winter, cold and all fish species love to huddle together under the low-lying branches of bankside trees. However, the fish are definitely going to react to that splash. It could be good: perhaps the fish are very torpid and the bait entry will jolt them into life, but if they're skittish it is far better to use much smaller balls.

coloured and cool a dead bait is always going to score. Freshwater dead baits are always good – and there is nothing a large pike likes better than a baby fish. Rainbow trout are also effective and can be bought direct from a fish farm or fishmonger. However, sea fish have,

◣ A DAY'S BAIT

These days, I'm going out on any piece of river or even a lake with just 20 or so pellets in my pocket. My thinking is this: I know exactly where the fish are lying and I know the pellets are devastatingly attractive to them. I can, therefore, bait with a single pellet, cast it out carefully to exactly the right spot and simply wait for a fish to make a mistake. I'll catch a fish and then move, so I'm always attacking shoals that are unspooked and unaware of my presence. You don't always need buckets of bait.

over the years, proved consistently successful, largely because of the scent and the oils they give off. Herring, mackerel, sprats, smelts and sardines all make excellent oily baits. When you are casting long distances, the softer ones, such as sardines, are best used still partly frozen so that they stay on.

Nowadays, wherever you live, artificial baits are available from world-wide manufacturers and the selection is astounding. Spinners and spoons, as simple as you can get, still work well. Plugs remain killers, be they floating, diving or surface-popping. Rubber jigs, fashioned to look like fish, frogs, lizards or whatever, can prove deadly in the hands of experts. The predator angler has, in short, never had it nearly so good, and modern lure fishing takes angling into new realms altogether. I said earlier that I'd be quite happy to use the ubiquitous lobworm for the rest of my fishing days: there would be many anglers equally content to have nothing in their bait box but small

rubber worms of different sizes and colours. Certainly, these will catch anything from the humblest minnow to the largest pike when put into the right hands. The world of lures is exciting and ever-changing.

◄ A TIMELY STRIKE
This pike was taken on a dead bait as you can see, and I particularly like the position of the bait itself. Remember that pike pick up their bait crosswise and then turn it so that it can be swallowed head first. The longer you delay the strike, the more likely the bait and the hooks will be down deep, and getting them out will be a messy job. As you can see, this bait hasn't been turned, which means the angler was alert and struck immediately there was an indication of a take.

⋏⋎ SENSITIVE RIGS
To hit a pike early your rig needs to be sensitive enough to indicate even the most gentle of takes. You can leger a bait effectively, but my favourite method is to use a float. Ensure that the depth is set with absolute accuracy so that any interest down at the bait end is registered on the float. Make sure, too, that you can see your float very clearly. Concentration is vital.

◄ UNDERNEATH THE ARCHES
Bridges nearly always attract fish and in large part this is because of food supplies. Look into the water and you will see the footings and buttresses of the construction – these are home to innumerable types of grubs and beetles. You'll also, almost certainly, find huge amounts of rubble around most bridges along with items of rubbish thrown in by passers-by. In time, these are all colonized by insects and the larder simply grows.

Choosing Intelligently

Bait is important. If a fish doesn't want the bait that you are offering, all the tackle and all the rigs imaginable will not persuade that fish to bite. All your patience and ingenuity and expense will be for nothing if what you have on the hook is suspect or unacceptable. The bait is probably the most central of all the aspects you have to bear in mind, but don't be frightened. You're always going to find something, and sometimes you can get too complicated.

In 1998, three friends and I went to the Czech Republic to fish for barbel. We took with us all manner of complex, hi-tech baits, and the barbel didn't recognize any single one of them as food. In the end, we simply resorted to turning over the rocks in the river and collecting a hundred or so caddis grubs for each day's fishing. Virtually every caddis grub would fetch a bite if fished intelligently. The barbel simply loved them. We had spent a fortune on bait that we might just as well have left at home. That's not always the case, but all too often it is: a simple solution can save the day.

Always keep your eyes open for any other clues along the bankside. For example, overhanging trees can often drop food items, such as baby birds or ripe fruit, into the water where they will be gobbled up by hungry fish. Anglers can exploit these forces of nature for their own means.

⋏ SEEK AND YOU SHALL FIND
I spend a great deal of time rooting around on banksides looking for natural baits. Remember that when a river floods huge quantities of terrestrial creatures are washed into the water and provide a hugely welcome food boost. Look for worms, slugs, beetles, leatherjackets – almost anything that creeps or crawls. Avoid creatures that are on endangered lists, such as, newts and do keep your eyes open for the sleeping, coiled serpent!

⋎ CADDIS GRUBS
Perhaps caddis grubs are safer and they're certainly easy to find. Search around in the margins of almost any river, pull up a decent-sized stone and you'll find caddis grubs glued to the underside. Simply squeeze a caddis out and you've got a superb bait for almost any fish that swims. Try mounting two or three caddis on a size 14. Never take more caddis, however, than you know you're going to use. Keep them alive and fresh in a bucket.

SKILLS

EXPERIENCE AND TIME SPENT AT THE WATERSIDE WILL BRING THE
GREATEST BENEFITS OF ALL. DON'T WORRY IF AT FIRST YOUR
APPROACH APPEARS CLUMSY, YOU GET INTO TANGLES OR IT TAKES YOU
AGES TO GET SET UP AND ACTUALLY STARTED. IF YOU'RE REASONABLY
DEXTROUS, ALL THE WRINKLES WILL BE IRONED OUT IN TIME AND
YOU WILL SOON ACHIEVE A 'SMOOTHNESS' IN EVERYTHING YOU DO.

It's easy to spot a well-practised angler: everything about him or her appears effortless: there's no rush, no panic and no uncertainty. There really is an art to fishing but, like everything, it's practice that makes for perfection.

There are physical gifts that make for angling success. Eyesight is vital: you won't be able to watch the tip of a float 40 yards away if you have less than good vision. If you have any doubts about your eyes, then get them checked, but you must also learn how to use them. Really watch what is going on around you at the waterside and try to make every event you witness count. All you see will fit into a complete picture. In nature, nothing happens randomly – there's a reason for everything.

To be a really excellent angler, you'll probably need what are referred to as 'soft hands'. This is much the same as a tennis player or a cricketer: if the racquet or bat is held stiffly, like an alien tool, then shots are not played fluently. It's just the same with that rod and reel. The idea is that they become an extension of your body and that you can use both without even thinking.

> AMERICAN DREAM
The three photographs on this spread all reflect my philosophy that to get the very best out of fishing you've got to physically get into the water as much as you possibly can and break down the barriers between you and the fish. In the colder waters of New York State, where this carp was caught, you've got to wear chest waders if you're going to get close to the fish.

Indeed if you're playing a big fish, for example, all your concentration has to focus on the battle and not on what your rod and reel are doing, which has to become second nature.

Don't ignore your physical fitness either. I'm not saying that you have to work out to be a successful fisherman, but the fitter you are, the more likely you are to explore distant stretches of river or the far end of the lake. Run out of puff and it's probable you won't go round that next bend to find the swim of your life. Of course, fishing itself can help keep you healthy. If you've walked, waded and fished over seven or eight miles of river through a 12-hour day, you deserve that meal at the end of it, a comfortable bed and a long sleep.

< GETTING IN THERE
Here you see my great friend Peter netting a carp in water knee deep. Peter frequently wades out deep to lay a carpet of bait.

Confident Casting

'Soft hands' are also vital when casting. You'll need to learn to 'feather' a cast by dabbing your finger on the spool as your float or lead nears its destination. This slows down the descent and allows the terminal tackle to land more gently in the water, and it can make the difference between success and failure. 'Soft hands' also allow you to flick a bait here and there with complete accuracy. Your casting won't fall short or end up over long in the overhanging bush.

Accurate casting is an art that comes through constant practice and experience of changing conditions. Wind, especially, can be the arch enemy, particularly if it's in your face and you are striving to make the desired distance with tackle that's too light. Don't try - use a heavier float or weight.

The right rod is essential for good casting. No matter how skilful you might be, you will never be able to cast if your gear is letting you down all the time. For example, it's no good striving to reach huge distances if you're only using a 6- or 7-foot rod. Equally, don't expect pinpoint accuracy of cast if your rod is 14 feet long. You've got to match the rod to the job ahead of you.

Similarly with your reel and line. Presuming you're using a fixed spool reel, make sure the line comes almost to the lip of the spool. If you don't have enough line on, or if that line is festooned with knots, you'll find casting distances severely limited. The distance you can cast with ease also depends to some degree on the diameter of that line: the thinner the line, the easier it will be to cast and control.

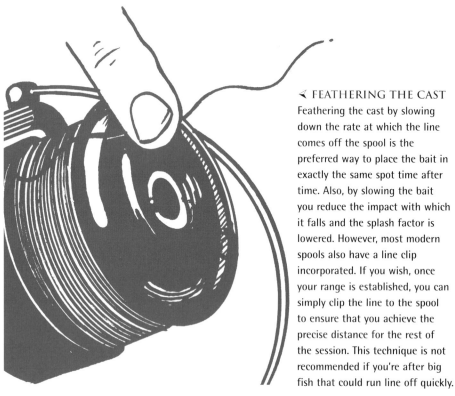

◄ FEATHERING THE CAST
Feathering the cast by slowing down the rate at which the line comes off the spool is the preferred way to place the bait in exactly the same spot time after time. Also, by slowing the bait you reduce the impact with which it falls and the splash factor is lowered. However, most modern spools also have a line clip incorporated. If you wish, once your range is established, you can simply clip the line to the spool to ensure that you achieve the precise distance for the rest of the session. This technique is not recommended if you're after big fish that could run line off quickly.

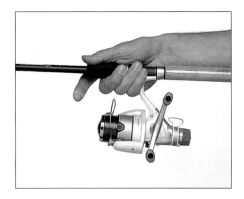

⋀ PREPARING TO CAST
Note the hand movements here as you're preparing to cast a bait out into the water. Make sure that the rod always feels comfortable in your hand, and see how the index finger is gripping the line so it won't fall off the spool when the bail arm is released.

⋀ SET TO GO
The line is now gripped tightly to the rod butt as the left hand moves back the bail arm. Once the bail arm is fully off, the line can flow off the spool freely. The cast can then be made by swinging the rod back, flicking it towards the target spot and releasing the line.

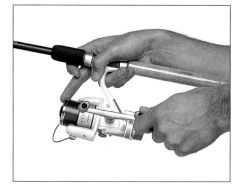

⋀ FEATHERING THE LINE
As the line flows off the reel, you may well want to slow the bait down as it threatens to overshoot the chosen target. Placing your finger on the spool allows you to do this. Once the cast is complete, turn the handle of the reel to flick the bail arm over the spool.

UNSNAGGING A WEEDED FISH

We all get weeded on occasion, however capable we are when it comes to playing a fish. The skill lies in getting the fish out of that weed. There are several useful approaches. The first is to let the line go completely slack for anything up to five minutes. Once the pressure is released, there's always a chance that the fish will think the danger is over and swim out the way it went in. Once you see the line begin to move, tighten up and start the battle anew.

Alternatively, change the angle of attack. Walk along the bank and try pulling in a different direction and you might find the fish comes free. If you're on a river, then get downstream of the fish and pull along with the flow of the

current. You'll find this frequently works, as you're pulling in the natural direction of the weed.

However, it may not work. The fish may be truly weeded and just won't come out. Now it's time for drastic action. Point your rod directly at the weeded fish and tighten up. It's important to gauge exactly how strong your line is at this point and how much pressure you can apply. Take the line in your left hand and begin to pull slowly backwards and forwards with a sawing motion. If you sense some give, reel in again and tighten up. Repeat the process. Eventually, with luck, you'll begin to feel the whole blockage on the move. The chances are you'll slowly reel in a great

clump of weed with a bemused fish buried in the middle!

Of course, you can avoid making life difficult for yourself from the word go. If you suspect a particular swim is festooned with snags, give it a miss – hooking a fish in these conditions isn't fair on anybody.

⋎ PINPOINT

It's not enough to get a bait in the water in the general direction of the fish. Ninety-nine times out of a hundred your cast has got to be pinpoint and your bait has to be lying in exactly the right position to get a take. This is why I've waded out to a rock so I can lower a bait precisely between two boulders a couple of yards from the rod tip. If I weren't as close, the current would simply catch the line and pull the bait out of position.

Good Timing

Timing is one of the critical factors in any cast and you must practise until you know instinctively when to raise your finger from the lip of the spool to allow the line to fly out. Raise that finger too soon and the cast will flop behind you: raise it too late and you'll simply thump the terminal tackle into the water in front of you. Practice will soon make perfect.

Above all, don't rush. Take your time and weigh all the factors affecting the cast: take into account the wind, where you want to put the bait and any obstructions either in the water or on the bankside behind you. I wonder how many of us have spent half the day retrieving tackle from overhanging trees! Before casting, make sure you are still, your rod is paused and your terminal tackle is hanging some three or four feet from the rod tip and is, again, perfectly motionless. Look to where you wish to cast, look at your terminal tackle, look again at the desired landing spot and flick the bait out towards it. Watch the terminal tackle in flight so that you know when to slow the line down by dabbing your finger on the reel spool. Aim above the water somewhat and the terminal tackle will fall with less of a splash. These are the basics, and it won't be long before you are getting it right.

⅄ WORK IT OUT

A gorgeous piece of water and it's tempting just to run to the bank, get fishing and cast in anywhere. Instead, regard the session like a chess game. Look at the water carefully and work out exactly where the fish might be. Look for deep runs close in or, if it's early morning, those gravelly shallows where fish will be hunting for food. Think exactly how the current is working and to where it will be pushing insects. There's a nice high bank here: take time to stand and watch for fish through polarizing glasses.

⋏ PRE-LAUNCH

Here's Peter again on his favourite carp lake. He has baited up at the 100-yard range and there are good numbers of carp out there feeding. Now's the time to get the bait out. A powerful 12- or 13-foot rod, a big reel loaded to the rim and a heavy enough weight are all necessary. Your line must be flawless because a big cast like this really piles on the pressure. Pete's stance is comfortable and relaxed and the rod is poised behind him, almost directly over his head. Everything is still now as Peter gauges exactly where he wants to put his bait and he prepares himself for the cast itself.

⋏ THE LAUNCH

Peter now sweeps the rod forward, bringing his forearms out in front of his face, his hands facing in the direction he wants to make the cast. The rod is gathering speed and the momentum will propel the bait through the air to the baited area. Although there's great power in this cast, Peter still maintains total control and is physically absolutely unflustered. His body position hasn't changed and he's obviously not physically straining. You can just see the terminal tackle in the top right of the photograph hanging about three to four feet from the rod tip itself – the perfect distance for maximum control.

⋏ RE-ENTRY

Once again, notice how Peter's body position is almost exactly the same throughout the three photographs. Look, too, at the position of his hands and the rod – still in the same true line to the feeding area. The bait is about to land and Peter is feathering its fall by controlling the line off the spool with his fingertip. By slowing the line down a little, the force of the cast is diluted and the bait enters with less of a splash. Once the bait hits the surface, Peter will keep the bail arm open so that line is given as the lead falls through the water. If he snaps the bail arm shut, then there'll be no free line and the bait will swing in back towards him in its descent.

Going for Distance

There are advanced casting techniques, of course. Nowadays, in the carp-fishing world especially, one of the overriding aims seems to be to put the bait as far away from the bank as possible. Casts of well over 100 yards are reportedly achievable. To do this, you obviously need the right rod, reel and line for the job. Terminal rigs, too, have to be quite sophisticated not to tangle in flight. The normal way is the overhead cast with the bait poised somewhere behind your backbone.

Your left hand clamps on the rod, but low down, and your right hand is over the reel with your finger controlling the line. The cast now should be a smooth, pendulum-like motion with an ever-increasing speed. Start with moderate distances first until you get the technique right, and don't strive for the horizon too early or you'll simply end up in tangles.

Also remember that the more effort you have to put into the cast then the more uneven the action will be and, again, the greater the

likelihood of a tangle. The important lesson to learn is that you won't be able to cast long distances unless you have exactly the right gear. If your rod is too short or under-powered, or if your reel is not large enough, or if your line is simply too thick then big distances are out of the question. And don't think that big fish always live at big distances. They don't. Only fish far if you know it's absolutely necessary and not to impress yourself or others.

Casting a Lure

Lure fishing is a very different game when you are frequently trying to cast a plug or spinner a short distance into a very tight area between weed or under overhanging branches. The underhand cast allows you to flick a lure into an opening beneath overhanging branches that would be difficult to reach from either side. If you're right-handed, try the backhand cast for placing the lure between branches that have an opening on the left-hand side. Try the forehand cast for flicking a lure under trees that have a way in on the right. In fact, you'll find that pinpoint accuracy is much more easily achieved with an underhand flick in this way than a cast over your shoulder. Once again, don't be alarmed – practice very quickly makes perfect.

⋏ IN THE JUNGLE

To get the best out of this under-fished lake, which is crowded with trees and reeds and there are no swims cut, you've got to wade from the margins and flick your plug here and there in the most likely 'piky' looking spots. Take care however: there's often a huge amount of silt in old lakes like this, so test each footstep before committing your whole weight.

➤ A SURFACE WORKER

Surface-working plugs often prove effective in jungle-like situations. In warm weather especially, predators lie near the surface to sun themselves, fully aware of what's going on around them. When the water is clear, shallow and calm the ripples made by a surface-crawling plug can be seen and felt from great distances. Work the plug erratically. Make it flip and flop across the water and then lie still. Pike will often hit it at moments of pause.

⋖ THE EXPLOSION

A pike has rocketed from underneath a tree to intercept the plug and it's hit it hard in the surface film. Now it cartwheels, head shaking, gills flaring, looking quite magnificent in the morning sunlight. The rod is forced down but fortunately I've got the clutch set lightly enough to give line and avoid a break off.

➤ BACK HE GOES

When you're in the water with the fish there's no need to take it onto the bankside. If the barbs are flattened then it's quite easy to keep the fish in the water and flick the hook points out with your forceps. Cradle the fish until it's ready to swim away.

Speciality Reels

So far I've generally talked about using a fixed-spool reel – centre pins and multipliers are marginally more complicated. The Wallis cast is a way of casting directly off a centre pin and it is mastered by so few I wouldn't worry about it unduly. Most centre pin situations don't call for long casting anyway, and a few yards of line can easily be drawn off the reel and held in the fingers of the free hand to allow shorter casts.

Multipliers should not really present a problem: most beginners go wrong either by buying a cheap multiplier that won't revolve particularly freely or by setting the reel up incorrectly. It's very important that the weight of the end tackle just causes the spool to revolve when the clutch is flicked off. If the terminal tackle doesn't cause the spool to revolve, then the drag on the spool is too great. If the spool revolves very fast, then the tension is set too lightly and a bird's nest is likely to result as the spool will overrun. Casting with a multiplier should, like all casting, be done in a rhythmical way. You're looking to use the rod like a pendulum, gradually picking up power as it goes. Once again, don't rush, take your time and keep cool.

Ambush Techniques

Children have great advantages over adults when it comes to ambush techniques. They are smaller so they are less easily seen and they are lighter so their footfall reverberates less through the water. But no matter how tall or heavy you are remember the lessons of infancy and try to make yourself as inconspicuous as possible in all fishing situations. Remember that in shallow, clear water especially fish can see us and our very clumsy approach very easily indeed. Approach every fishing situation with caution and make every bit of use of natural cover that you can. Capitalize on natural disturbances. For example, if cattle are drinking use the commotion they make to get yourself down to the waterside unnoticed. If swans are fighting, now is a good time to introduce some ground bait…

⅄ ON YOUR STOMACH
Robin and Al aren't at all afraid to lie for an hour or more on their stomachs, close to a shallow pool where they can watch the fish but remain unseen themselves.

⅄ IN THE RUSHES
Tim's out of the water but wants to make himself invisible. He screens himself behind last year's bulrushes so he can get close to the fish without spooking them.

◄ FISH ON

The float has gone under, Henry has struck and a good-sized barbel is heading off down river. The rod's a long one but it's got plenty of power and the choice of reel is a centre pin. At this stage in the fight there's not much Henry can do but keep direct control and let the pin spin to the force of the run.

⅋ SIDE STRAIN

The first mad rush of the fish is beginning to slow but Henry is worried. The barbel has got close to some big rocks and if he gets round them the line will grate and probably part. Notice now Henry swings the rod over to the right to put a different angle of pressure on the fish. This, he hopes, will pull the barbel's head round and swing it off course.

Playing the Fish

Playing a fish should be extremely exciting, especially when you have a fish on the line that can really bend the rod and make your reel clutch screech. Herein lies the first lesson: don't set that clutch too tight.

⅋ GONE TOO FAR

The plan worked and the barbel was deflected from the rocks. The trouble is, the force of Henry's side strain pulled it towards some overhanging trees – more trouble. As a result, Henry's got to swing the rod 180 degrees and really pile the pressure on to keep the barbel from this second danger.

Modern clutches are excellent and reliable and you can use them with impunity provided that they are set right in the first place. As a rough guide, hold the line in one hand and pull against it until the rod bends into a quarter circle. At this stage the clutch should begin to give line.

Obviously, for really tight, snaggy conditions you are going to have to tighten up to a degree or the fish will achieve sanctuary. In my view, it's better to go a little slack: you can always tighten up later, whereas if you're too tight to begin with, you may not get a second chance!

⍌ THE CRITICAL MOMENT
Henry's done 90 per cent of the job here and the barbel is tired, beaten and on its side. However, there's probably still enough power in there for a final surge. Notice how Henry keeps his rod high at this stage so it can absorb any last-minute frantic antics!

⍃ KEEP IT COMING
The two side strain attacks worked and now Henry is working the fish back upriver towards him. He's using the pumping technique – drawing the fish through the water and then lowering the rod and reeling quickly to take up the slack line. Once a fish is coming, you've got to keep it on the move. Don't relax, don't give it time to regroup, dig in and go on another run.

Keep It Up!

When you're playing a fish, always keep the rod up so that it can cushion the plunges of the fish, somewhat like a shock absorber. If you point the rod more directly at the fish, then the forgiving flexibility is lost.

Pumping is an important skill and is particularly useful for bigger fish, which can be very difficult to lift off the bottom. Starting with the rod in a near-vertical position you lower it towards the fish, reeling in rapidly, but in complete control, until your rod tip is close to the water's surface. Then, making sure the clutch is set reasonably tight on your reel, you gently and steadily move the rod back to the vertical, pulling the fish upwards through the water towards you. Keep repeating the process until the fish is close enough to net or beach, but always be aware of what the fish is doing. If you sense that it's preparing for a run then hold steady and be ready to give line if necessary.

A lot of mistakes are made when the fish is close to the bank. They will frequently make a last surging run, so make sure the rod is held high and the clutch is set reasonably slackly to accommodate this. Draw the fish to the waiting net and don't chase it. The more you splash around with the net, the more the fish will be alarmed and the greater the chance of an accident. It also makes sense to keep low against the skyline so that the fish sees as little of you as possible.

The most important message when playing any fish is that your gear is sound in the first place and strong enough for the job you have in mind. There's no point in hooking a fish just for it to break free.

⍌ HELD FOR A SECOND
This beautiful fish, which was around the ten-pound mark, is held for a second in the bright sun and then released with no harm done.

PRACTICE

ALL THE PREPARATION IS OVER AND THE BUZZ WORD NOW IS 'GO', BUT DON'T RUSH IN. ALL YOUR MOVEMENTS MUST BE CONTROLLED. WHETHER IT'S WADING, CASTING OR PLAYING A FISH, DO EVERYTHING CALMLY. FISHING IS ALL ABOUT KEEPING A COOL HEAD AND SENSITIVE HANDS. LOSE CONTROL AND YOUR GAME WILL SIMPLY GO TO PIECES.

TACKLING RIVERS

YOU CAN APPROACH RIVERS IN ONE OF TWO PRINCIPAL WAYS – BY REMAINING STATIC OR BY BEING MOBILE. IF YOUR RIVER IS HEAVILY FISHED AND THE BANKS ARE LINED WITH ANGLERS THEN YOU HAVEN'T GOT MUCH CHOICE IN THE MATTER. IF, HOWEVER, YOUR RIVER HAS LARGE AREAS OF COMPARATIVELY UNPRESSURED WATER THEN YOU DO HAVE THE OPTION TO ROAM, SO DO SO.

Whether you're a roamer or a stayer, the most important thing is not to spook the fish. If the fish are scared, then they'll either stop feeding or just vanish. This goes for fish everywhere, no matter what the water type. However, what I'm going to say now is particularly important on rivers, because they are generally quite small and the fish are close to you. Consider these rules and don't scotch your chances before you even cast out.

Remember that noise carries approximately five times further in water than it does in air. This means that anything splashing through the water's surface or any undue disturbance on the bankside can be heard for long distances. A heron doesn't keep itself fed by being noisy.

Consider everything: keep your movements subdued, controlled and to a minimum. Keep your shadow off the water, and try not to stand out on the horizon. Make sure your clothing merges into the background as much as possible. Everything counts: if your arrival startles waterfowl, for example, they'll panic and splash across the water, taking your chances of success with them.

Dawn is often a cracking good time to be out on the river, largely because no one else has been there before you. It's good if there's dew, or even frost, on the bankside, because the telltale footsteps show whether your swim has already been fished that day, as any previous disturbance really will scupper the fishing.

High banks are excellent both to fish from and as vantage points. Provided that you keep your shadow down, fish find it more difficult to see you when you're relatively high above them.

➤ A NET SOMETIMES

If you're at all worried about bringing a fish to hand then a net obviously does the job. Bring the fish over the net so that it's safe but you can still unhook it in the water so that there's no pressure on the fish's flanks. Notice how I'm crouching: the less the fish sees of me at this stage of the fight, the less likely it is to make a final surge.

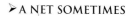

◀ A PERFECT PLAN

Rob and Kerry have noticed some feeding fish downstream of this large bush. It would be no good fishing from the bank because presentation would be destroyed by the flow of the river. By getting out there, Kerry can fish right down the force of the current and have little bow in his line. This means that he can use a light weight that won't disturb the fish. By standing close into the bush the profile of both men is masked.

⋏ NO FEAR

Brian has seen a magnificent bit of river and has already scaled a cliff to get there. Now he's climbing an eight-foot deer fence to get to the water itself. He went on to catch eight fish in 90 minutes, so the effort was justified. Consider being physically fit and travelling light. If you can get to the places that others can't then you can enjoy sessions of a lifetime.

⋏ THE ROAMER

And here comes Brian again, climbing back up the cliff after his wildly successful session. If you are pushing the boundaries like this, make sure that you possess the right footwear. You don't want to be scrabbling for a foothold in situations like this. Be careful with that rod too. Sometimes it is best to walk with the tip behind you in case you do fall or stumble.

Grass and mud banksides are much better than gravel. If you've got to fish on gravel, walk as though you're on hot coals. (For this reason, I much prefer touch legering to standard quiver tipping: just forcing a rod rest into gravel can be disastrous.)

Look for steady runs of water close in. If you're not fishing at a distance, it's much easier to place loose feed into the water without any splash whatsoever. Better still, wade into the water and place your loose feed under the surface by hand to rule out the splash factor altogether. Wading is good news if you don't crunch your feet, and fish aren't as

⋖ UNDER THE ROD TIP

Polaroid glasses have picked up some big fish feeding in close in around four to five feet of water. The approach is simple: creep into position, fish on your knees and keep a rod length's distance between yourself and the water. Remember that if you wave the rod tip out over the top of feeding fish there's every chance that they will pick up on it and flee.

afraid of you when you're actually in the water with them. As an added bonus, stirred up silt helps mask your tackle and draws in small fish to feed on the dislodged food items… and small fish feeding inspire the bigger ones to do the same.

Watch out for any natural disturbance on the water and use this to your benefit. For example, if a canoe or a group of swans paddles past, or if cattle come down to feed, use the disturbance to put in a cast.

Whether you're fishing a feeder or a straight lead, use as light a weight as you can possibly get away with, to minimize the splash. I can't overstate how important it is to make that very first cast an absolutely critical one, precisely because of the splash factor. Don't waste it by using it to check out the depth or the speed of the current – it diminishes your efficiency.

Take all these points seriously, please. The fish you're after in rivers are wild creatures, and in order to

survive they've honed their senses to an incredible degree. You're only fooling yourself if you fail to take this into account.

⅄ FLOAT CONTROL

I can't emphasize enough how important it is to fish with the current rather than across it. Here you see Phil trotting a float along a quick piece of water. Notice how his rod is held out over the river so that the tip can follow the line of the float precisely. This way there's little or no chance that the current can catch the line and pull the float off its true, intended course.

◅ THE MARGINS

If your approach to the river is painstaking you'll be amazed how often you will find fish coming into the shallows to feed. If you've got 'skinny' water in front of you, then try putting out a bait with no lead whatsoever. Something heavy like lobworm, a small fish or a piece of breadflake or cheese will hold bottom if the current isn't too strong. All the lead would do is create extra splash and probably alarm the fish.

The Static Approach

If you're going to fish just one swim, have a good reason for doing so, and not just laziness or lack of confidence in other areas. It's always good to experiment with new swims.

If you decide to fish just the one spot make sure that it's the right one, especially if you're new to the river. Local knowledge plays some part, but bear in mind that if you've plumped for a favourite swim the spot will be pressured and the fish will be wary. Perhaps you can see the fish: that's great and it makes for exciting fishing. Fine, but do understand that the fish don't always conform to the textbooks.

⅄ UPSTREAM LEGERING

Remember that you don't always have to leger downstream or across, as upstreaming like this can be hugely effective. You need less lead to hold bottom and the fish feel very little resistance when they pick up the bait. What you're likely to experience is a quick jab and then the line falling slack. Strike at once.

⅄ HUGE POTENTIAL

There are times when the static approach is absolutely essential, such as on large waters like this when fish populations aren't particularly high. You've simply got to lay an ambush and sit it out. The sun sinks and night is just minutes away. The fish will certainly be on the move and the action could start at any moment.

73

Legering

You've got to decide on your approach and your bait. If you're going to spend a whole day here, then it's probable that small baits in big quantities are going to work best. Think maggots, casters, small pellets, hemp seed and perhaps sweetcorn – maybe coloured red or black, especially in these pressured days.

Next you've got to think how to introduce this bait: do you catapult or throw it out, or spread it by means of a swim feeder or bait dropper? Bait droppers are great for close-in work, and feeders have caught fish now for decades at greater ranges. So, for that reason, most anglers go for swim feeders allied with quiver tips for bite indication. This standard approach often works, especially on heavily stocked waters where there is strong competition for food. Over the day, or so the theory goes, you get the

⋏ THE FEEDER

The feeder obviously gets samples of bait to the bottom in close vicinity to the hook. It can, therefore, be a useful tool but be careful in shallow, clear water where the splash of entry is a problem and where it's very obvious. The feeder, too, is more likely to work with naïve than pressured fish.

⋎ GENTLE RELEASE

This barbel is being held in the current until its strength is fully returned to swim away safely. Otherwise it would simply be swept away, turned belly up and, in all probability, drown. Remember, too, that the less time any fish spends out of the water the shorter the recuperation time needed.

fish more and more preoccupied with your baits and the bites become more and more frequent. The theory often works in practice, but don't be too complacent. If there aren't that many fish, or if they're at all spooky, then you'll find the continual splash of the swim feeder unsettles them even more. Also, in cold weather the fish are much more likely to eat sparingly and just the odd, attractive, smelly bait is more likely to be taken.

Choose your swim feeder carefully: you want it to be just heavy enough to hold bottom but light enough to dislodge the moment the fish lifts the bait. Don't use swim feeders that are too garish in colour – they stand out like a sore thumb on the riverbed. If it's cold weather, maggots won't come out of the swim feeder quickly enough, so be prepared to enlarge the holes with a pair of scissors if necessary.

Think carefully about your main line: swim feeder fishing puts a lot of strain on it and you shouldn't go too light – six-pound breaking strain would be my minimum choice. Hook lengths can be scaled down, but only if you're quite sure of both the size of the fish in front of you and the number of snags. Don't leave hooks in fish as a matter of course. It's just not fair. Choose to go for fewer bites and more fish landed.

Heavier lines also give you far more control over any fish during the fight. This is important, as if you don't have confidence in your line you'll let the fish dictate the battle, and this very often ends in disaster.

⋏ A SUNSET BARBEL
There'll always be occasions where you want a photograph in an out-of-water setting. In this particular case, John was fishing from a very steep bank where it was unsafe to wade. The only possibility was to actually land the fish and pose for a quick photograph.

⋎ THE FEEDER IN ACTION
This shot shows how and why feeders work. It was taken about six feet down in a quick-moving river and the only way to get a consignment of maggots down to the bed in such tight formation is with the feeder approach. I'm not happy about that shiny snap-link that the angler has used, however.

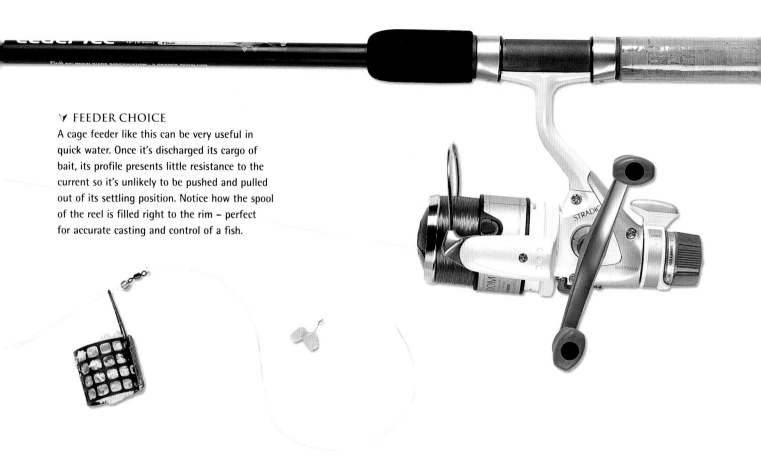

⩔ FEEDER CHOICE

A cage feeder like this can be very useful in quick water. Once it's discharged its cargo of bait, its profile presents little resistance to the current so it's unlikely to be pushed and pulled out of its settling position. Notice how the spool of the reel is filled right to the rim – perfect for accurate casting and control of a fish.

Think carefully about your hook length: do you use braid or mono? My advice would be mono for sheer predictability. How long should your hook length be? You can make it longer in very slow water, but in fast water go for a short hook length of no more than 8 inches or the current will tend to lift the bait up and make it behave like a mini-propeller in the water.

Pitch your rod rest so that the rod remains high and there is as little line as possible in the water. Bites on

⩔ VIRGIN WATER

This is a shot of a river where the feeder has, to my knowledge, never been used. On water like this the feeder can have a truly killing effect. The fish don't associate it yet with danger. This is a very juicy bit of water: explore the area between the clear and coloured water, a phenomenon that all fish adore.

the quiver tip can be anywhere in the range from a slight knocking or trembling to a full-blooded lunge. Be aware and strike anything that looks positive, but if in doubt don't strike, because a feeder flying up from the bottom invariably unsettles the fish in the swim. Carry a choice of different coloured quiver tips so you always have perfect visibility against any backdrop.

Consider very carefully how much bait you want to put into a swim and how regularly you are going to cast. There are no hard and fast rules, but if you are getting no indication of activity on the tip I would suggest you slow up a bit. If bites keep crashing your rod over, then you can afford to put more and more bait in, safe in the knowledge that there are a good number of fish out there feeding hard.

Part of the swim feeder's art is to know what size of hook to use: generally it pays to go as small and light as you can, taking into consideration both the bait and the size and power of the fish in front of you. If you're using maggots or casters, then a size 14 with three bait items is a good starting point. Two grains of sweetcorn on a size 10 harmonize well. If you're struggling, try unusual baits – lobworms or cheese paste, for example. Give the fish something they haven't seen often and you could get an instant response.

▷ MULTIPLE BAITS

The river is up and flowing and visibility is very poor. Any fish that you might catch is going to be hunting by smell rather than sight and this is when a multiple bait can really score heavily. With a baiting needle, thread three chunks of luncheon meat up the line, tie on the hook – a large one, say size 2 or 4 – and then slide the meat back down the line, the bottom piece settling over the shank of the hook. Make sure always that the hook point is exposed for a clean, efficient strike.

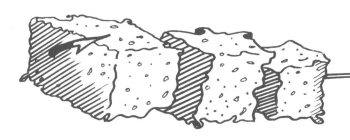

▽ RING THE CHANGES

When the water clears out somewhat, then perhaps two pieces of meat are all that you're going to need. If they're getting very finicky then only a tiny, single piece will be needed.

Remember, also, that fish will become suspicious of the cubed shape. If you suspect this, simply rip a piece of ragged meat off and hook that. This also has the advantage of dribbling little pieces into the current which attract fish in.

PROBLEM BUSTING

'I only get odd plucks and nibbles from small fish and never a proper pull.'

• Try a radical, surprise bait. If you've been using small, go big, and vice versa. Try a cocktail: two maggots and a sliver of meat on a size 12 hook. Go enormous: three large pieces of luncheon meat perhaps threaded on the hook and up the line. Go natural: turn over some stones in the margin and see if you can find any caddis grubs. Try three on a size 12 hook.
• Look at your hook length and change it. In fast water perhaps you ought to go shorter. If the pace of the current is slow try lengthening it by three or four inches each cast. Don't be tempted to go lighter – you could simply lose a good fish.
• Try a new swim. It could just be that there aren't any big fish where you are.

Give your first cast half an hour and if there's no indication move swim again until you find yourself onto fish.
• Don't always think that these plucks and quivers that you're experiencing, either on the quiver tip or when touch legering, must be small fish. If they're at all irregular and come out of nothing and then disappear, the chances are that they are big fish being wary.

➤ CAREFUL SHOTTING

It's imperative that whatever float you use is shotted precisely. Ideally, you will just be able to see the tip of a float as it trickles down the river away from you. This is a stick float, very sensitive and ideal for using with smaller baits. Bites will generally be registered by a quick jab as the float buries; occasionally it will rise in the water.

Float Fishing

There are all manner of ways that you can use a float in moving water. If you really want to search a river then you can't beat long trotting. A buoyant, Avon-type float that sits reasonably proud of the water can carry your bait up to 100 yards away and still be visible. To control your tackle at this sort of range you'll need comparatively light line that floats well. Also, go for a reasonably powerful rod about 13 feet long. Make sure you have plenty of line on your spool! There are many arts to long trotting, but one of the main ones is making sure that you mend the line and keep it as straight and direct to the float as possible. If you let the currents push the line here and there you'll have absolutely no contact whatsoever if you eventually get a bite. Just as bad is unmended line that hangs in the current and pulls the float completely off course, usually burying it in the marginal weed just a few yards away from you.

As soon as you see a bite, hit hard and keep the rod sweeping back. You often only make contact right at the end when the float is a long way off. Try, if you can, to hustle the fish

➤ THE BITE

The stick float buries, pulled under by a quick-biting fish. This is actually the underwater view of what happens and notice the explosion of light around it – very off-putting for a shoal of fish in shallow, clear water. Don't, therefore, strike if you're not absolutely sure that it is a bite. It's far better to miss a fish than to disturb the entire swim.

from the shoal, although this can be difficult with anything like a largish chub at such long distances. Once you've located the fish by long trotting, you know where they are and you can move down to get closer to them, but again watch how you do that and don't spook them.

If you know where the fish are then you can get to them with a smaller float, often a stick float allied with a reasonably small bait such as maggots or casters. The float is shotted all the way down the line and the key here is to hold the float back so that it doesn't over-run the bait, as the current is nearly always quicker nearer the surface than it is at the bottom. By holding the float back you also make the bait rise slightly and this entices the fish into frequent mistakes. Another advantage of holding the float back is that the first thing the fish sees is the bait and not the line or the shot, which is terribly important in clear water and a good light.

➤ OVER-DEPTH TROTTING
Attach a float top and bottom and set well over depth – in quick water even twice the depth is not too much. Let the float work its way down the swim, little by little, holding it back for a minute before letting it on its way again.

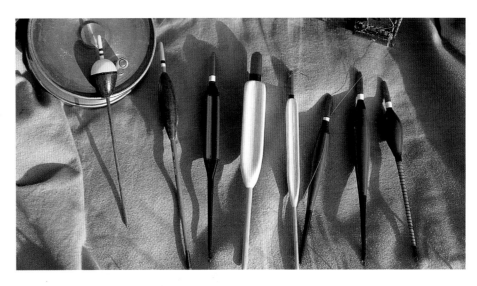

⚰ RIVER FLOATS
All of these river floats have, to some degree or another, bulked bodies to allow them to fight against the current and not be pushed under easily. The float on the extreme left is an old-fashioned bob float, but it still has its uses in very shallow, very rapid water. Notice, too, the three floats with fluted stems in the middle of the picture. Bodies shaped like this give the float great stability in heavy currents and allow you to mend the line successfully without pulling them a jot off course. All these floats are attached by two pieces of rubber band at the bottom and the top of the body. Practise shotting them to perfection in dead water so that when you make your first cast to the fish everything rides just as you expect down the current.

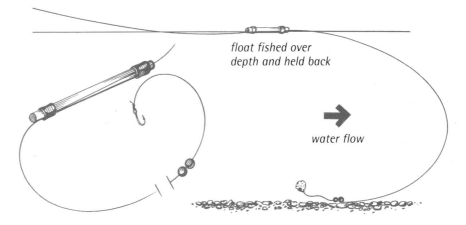

float fished over
depth and held back

water flow

PROBLEM BUSTING

'I'm long trotting and having problems with my float control... it just seems to be all over the place and not following a proper course down the river.'

Firstly, check out your tackle. Is your rod long enough? A 12-foot rod is really the minimum for float fishing. Is your line fine enough and, importantly, is it floating? Heavy, sinking line is bound to pull the float off course. Are you using the right float? There's no point in using a thin, delicate waggler in streamy water. Is your float big enough? You've got to put a bit of pressure on it to keep mending the line successfully, and you don't want to pull it off course.

The wind can make life difficult, too. An upstream wind isn't generally a problem, but a downstream one is a killer, and any wind blowing across, especially if it's strong, can blow the float out of true.

Don't be too ambitious at first – restrict yourself to reasonable distances. It's not realistic to be straining for 100 yards on your first day out.

Look for the right water. To begin with, choose a stretch that's neither too deep nor too fast. Remember that extreme depth and speed are two of the biggest problems when it comes to operating a float successfully. Like any skill, trotting a float is one that builds with experience.

◄ SEARCHING THE RIVER

The great beauty of trotting is that you can let the float go anything up to a hundred yards to search out the fish for you. If you wade out into the river you will find your control is immaculate. If you do get bites at a very long distance then mark the spot, creep slowly into place and fish more tightly and accurately. Trotting is particularly good when you're not sure exactly where the fish are going to be lying or you are on a water that is new to you.

You can also use a float set way over depth to let the current catch the loop of line between the float and bait and gently move the whole rig down the river, searching out fish as it goes. It's a good plan for bottom-feeding

▼ A PEARL OF NATURE

A mint perfect roach and the float that caught it. Roach are frequently very shy-biting fish and the float is the perfect indicator. Tackle them with tiny baits, such as maggots, casters or hemp seed, and you'll see bites that you'd miss altogether on a quiver tip.

fish where there aren't many snags about. Bites tend to be very positive.

Never try to fish with a float that's too light for the power of the river: it's better to go with one too big than one too small, because if it's always being pulled under you won't know whether it's the bite or the power of the river. Continued false striking simply spooks the fish. A variety of different coloured float tops is also important, especially when sighting is critical on a long trot down.

▼ HOLDING BACK

Holding the float back is one of the great art forms of trotting. Remember that the current is faster at the top of the water than at the bottom, so if the float is allowed to drift down uncontrolled it will pull the bait along at an unnatural speed. By slowing the float you make it move at the speed of the water deep down. It's a good idea to even stop the float from time to time. This has the effect of lifting the bait off the bottom a little so that it is the first thing that the fish sees. This way the line and the lead become much less obvious and shy fish are more tempted to bite.

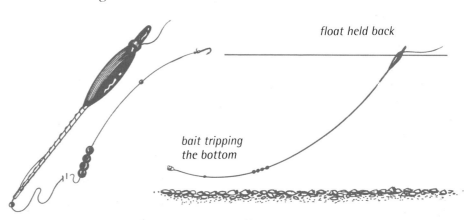

float held back

bait tripping the bottom

Mobile River Fishing

My perfect day is to cover five or six miles of river, possibly fishing some 30 different swims. I'll pop in on known swims and some that I've never fished before and know nothing about. I'll travel very, very light with a small pouch of baits, a light rod and reel, some hooks, some leads and that's about it. I won't even take a landing net, because most of the time I'll be wading and I can simply draw the fish into the shallows where I'm standing and flick out the barbless or semi-barbed hook with just a twist of the forceps.

In all probability, I won't put any loose feed in whatsoever and I certainly won't use a swim feeder.

I'll be legering with as small a lead as I can get away with, and I'll make that first cast count each and every time. Why won't I be using any loose feed? Simply because I'll be fishing exactly where I think the fish are and I'll be giving them a bait that I hope they can't resist, so why run the risk of spooking them by putting loose feed in when it isn't really necessary?

For bait, and this is critical, I'll choose whatever I'm sure the river is really switched onto at any given period (see Switched On Rivers, opposite). It could be sweetcorn, it could be pellets, it could be paste, lobworms, bunches of maggots or even dead minnows. The important

⋏ LONG TROTTING
You'll notice the size of the float that I'm using here. It is big because it's carrying a heavy weight and I want to be able to see it at great distances. I'm actually fishing for chub and these can be very spooky if you get closer than fifty or sixty yards. It's important that your line floats when fishing such big distances or you won't be able to pick it up on the strike. Either grease it or buy one of the specifically designed float fishing lines.

thing is that I'll have complete confidence in the bait and I'll fish each swim with absolute intensity.

If I haven't had a bite after two or three casts, I'll simply move on. In fact, I'll move on anyway, even if I do catch a fish. That's the whole pleasure of being mobile: you take a fish and move. That way you don't stress the river and you learn more about it each and every trip.

I certainly won't be carrying a rod rest, because I won't be using a quiver tip. I'll be touch legering always, in virtually all river types and for all fish species. It's customary nowadays to use a 12-foot rod for bigger fish such as chub and barbel, but I prefer something about 9 feet long – generally marketed as a spinning-type rod. I find this light and responsive, and it will play a big fish very happily indeed. A shorter rod is also very useful if you've got to push through heavy jungle along the riverbanks. It goes without saying that I'll be wearing my chest waders, although I won't enter the water if it's deep, coloured or dangerous.

➤ A NEW RIVER

There's nothing more exciting than your first few casts in a totally unexplored piece of water. This particular river gushes through central Spain, and talk about a place oozing promise... the trouble is none of us got a single bite so never go on appearances alone!

SWITCHED ON RIVERS

All fish go through periods of trying baits out, liking what they taste, getting caught on them and then becoming afraid and switching off them. But how do you know which baits are on or off in any particular river at any particular time? What is the river switched on to?

If you can see fish and their reaction to baits in clear water, whether running or still, you stand a great chance. If a bait is on, you will see that fish come among the particles, go down on them immediately and move slowly through them, browsing as they go. They will often dig deep, sending up bubbles, which are further proof that the fish are feeding confidently.

If you can see the fish and they are approaching the bait in a very hesitant way, then you should have your doubts about the bait. You might see them come repeatedly to a bait, stop a hand's length away and then back off. In extreme cases they will just bolt.

If you're quiver-tip fishing or touch legering you will experience quick, short pulls as the fish pick bait up, hold it in their lips for a second and then put it quickly back down again. This is a typical reaction from fish that are wary of a bait. Occasionally there are huge pulls. These are from fish that are scared and that is why they are picking

up a bait and then bolting with it in terror.

You know a bait is on when you get bites that are slow, solid and unmissable. There are no flicks, plucks or wild, hammering bites – just confident measured ones that are difficult to miss.

If a bait is becoming 'blown' or recognized, then you can try dying or flavouring it to give it a bit more life. Sweetcorn, for example, can be reinvented by colouring it red or black.

The safest thing to do is to switch to a new bait altogether. If at all possible try to feed this bait into a good number of swims before trying it on the hook.

The Thrill of Touch Legering

Let me give you one or two concrete examples… it's 8am and I'm making a start. I come to a long glide with deep water some two-thirds of the way across the river. I've got my polarizing sunglasses on and I look for any fish moving, but I can't see anything. Nonetheless, experience tells me there will be fish out there. I weigh up the strength of the current and decide that just a small lead will hold bottom. I use a hook length of some 15 inches because the water isn't too pacy, and I put a large, smelly pellet onto the hook by means of an elastic band. I then cast slightly upstream and let the bait fall to the bottom but maintain direct contact all the time. I then make sure the rod tip is pointing as directly towards where I think the bait is lying as I possibly can. I make sure everything is tight – just tightening up with another turn of the reel would force the lead to roll downstream – and then I take the line between the reel and the first rod ring between my fingers. I'll often just loop it over my first finger for sensitivity.

I'm feeling for anything that the river and the fish might tell me. Sometimes I'll get line bites – the bodies and the fins of fish brushing against the line. Occasionally I can

feel the bait being gently picked up and put down again and never properly taken. At other times I'll feel small tugs and then a longer one and – strike! Once in a while I'll strike without knowing precisely why – it's just like magic. Sometimes just a steady build up in pressure will signify a bite. Now and then the lead will be dislodged, bounced downstream half a yard, and then there'll be a tug. It's impossible to say exactly what a bite is going to feel like but, believe me, when you're holding that line, somehow you'll

⋏ TOUCH LEGERING
Touch legering is as exciting a method as there is. Your fingers can tell you just as much as your eyes but, as ever, practice makes perfect. It's all a matter of confidence: feel that first bite, strike successfully and you really know that what seems like magic is actually a truly practical proposition.

know. You'll just be aware that there's a living creature at the other end and it's taken your bait. In fact, that's my biggest kick of all. After the bite and the sheer adrenaline of it everything else is secondary.

Let's take a look at another swim about a mile lower down. It's very slack here, just downstream of a large overhanging tree. I can actually get away with hardly any weight at all, just one SSG a couple of feet up from the hook to give a bit

➢ CONCENTRATION
Giles has been touch legering for half his life now and he knows that concentration is vital to the method. But look how easily he is standing, the rod tucked under his arm, his fingers telling him exactly what's happening down there around the bait. Notice, too, the broad-peaked cap – very useful for taking the glare off the water.

PROBLEM BUSTING

'I like the idea of touch legering but I can never seem to get comfortable.'

Firstly, make sure your rod and reel aren't too heavy for you. Go for lightness and directness all the time. Make sure you're sitting or, more often, standing completely at ease and wholly comfortable. Hold your rod with your fingers round the reel seating and make

sure that the butt tucks comfortably under your shoulder.

Feel free and relaxed and simply experiment with different positions. If you're sitting, you can rest your non-rod hand on your knee as you hold the line. This gives added control.

Above all, play it cool and don't feel uptight or restricted. Just chill out and you'll soon find the right position.

of tension for the touch legering technique. I flick the bait in with an underhand swing so that there's hardly any splash at all and, once again, I try to keep the contact as direct as possible. This time there's absolutely no doubting a bite whatsoever – the rod's nearly pulled from my hands and I find I'm playing a smashing barbel within five minutes of settling down.

Touch legering has so much to commend it: the knowledge that the line gives you; the excitement of the bite itself. Even if you're not getting true bites, line bites will often show there are fish in the swim. You don't have to watch a float or a quiver tip, so you can look up and down the river for feeding fish. It's a great method at night because nothing is visual and everything is tactile. You can even day-dream if you like and you'll still be fishing effectively.

⅄ DANCING STREAMS
Rivers are all about life and vitality and a weir pool, like this, is a feature no angler can ever overlook. Fishing close to pounding water is always a good idea for many reasons, one of the most overlooked being that the constant noise of the crashing water masks your own fishing approach.

⅄ USE YOUR LOAF
Bread really is one of the most adaptable baits around, and although it can be made into a paste, I still prefer it in its simplest flake form. In an ideal world, don't use too much lead when fishing flake because you want it to fall as naturally and slowly as possible.

PROBLEM BUSTING

'I love the floating crust method, but the chub always come short on my river and only take loose offerings and not the one on the hook.'

Are you sure that you're mending the line effectively so that the crust isn't being pulled around unnaturally by the current? If your line is too heavy you will find this a problem, but don't go too fine and risk a break. Make sure that the last couple of yards of line to the crust is actually sinking. The chub find it more difficult to pick out a line when it's not on the surface.

Try crusts of different sizes... go big and then small until you find an answer.

Let's get really cunning: tie or fix a piece of crust onto your line about eight inches or so above the hook. Sometimes you can simply thread the line through and hold it with leger stops placed above and below the crust and wedged in firmly.

Now here comes the cunning bit: on the hook itself put a piece of breadflake that has been squeezed so that it just sinks. The chub comes to the crust, spooks but picks up the flake as it turns away – or at least that's the idea!

Let's get even more cunning! Tie a piece of twig or a feather above the hook so that it lies snug to the line. You'll find this breaks up the profile of the line and can fool the chub completely.

⅄ CUNNING IN THE EXTREME
The line is pushed through the flake with a baiting needle, then the hook is tied on and the flake baited. It's often also a good idea to have your line sunk so that it doesn't form a silhouette on the surface. You can vary the distance between the crust and the slowly sinking flake. Around about six inches to a foot is ideal. Watch the crust being pulled under or across the current as a bite indicator.

Surface Fishing

This is a great method if you're on a new river and you're hunting out chub in particular. The species are absolute gluttons for surface baits and, providing the water is reasonably clear, they'll come a good 5 or 6 feet off the bottom to intercept crusts floating overhead.

You need a large, white, unsliced loaf for this job. Pull off some 15 small pieces and throw them well out into mid-river and then sit back and watch their journey as they head downstream. Binoculars help. They might go 5, 50 or 500 yards before they're taken. You might see bow waves coming across the river after them, followed by big splashes – or you might see nothing and have to move on.

Once you do locate chub feeding hard like this, get reasonably close – say 10 to 30 yards away. You'll need just a rod, reel, 5-lb breaking strain line and a hook – nothing else at all. Take a size 4 hook and put on a small chunk of bread about the size of your thumb. It often pays to push the hook through the white bread and out of the crust. Loop the line round once or even twice and then push the hook back over the line into the bread again. You'll find this makes it stay on just that little bit more securely.

Dunk the bread lightly in the water in the margins to give it weight and then just flick it out into the current so that it follows the route of the free offerings. Make sure the line is mended carefully so that the current doesn't drag the crust off course… the chub will immediately be suspicious if it is.

Is that a take? Yes, but don't strike prematurely. Wait for the line to zip across the surface and tighten thoroughly before you sweep the rod back gently but powerfully. Is there a more satisfying, exciting way of catching chub? I doubt it. Is there a better way of locating chub on a river that you don't know? Definitely not.

⅄ OFF THE TOP

A chub comes up and sucks in a large piece of flake. It is tempting to strike at once, but don't. Very often a fish will just suck in the bait and hang there for a good few seconds before moving off with it. Wait for the line to tighten and pull across the current before sweeping the rod back to make contact.

◁ THE SHALLOWS
Here you see a wild, brown trout over the gravel that is kept clean by the quick-flowing water of the rapids.

THE BACK EDDY

Back eddies are generally deep and always sheltered from the main flow of the current. The water swings slowly round and round in a gentle rhythmic motion. Back eddies aren't used much in normal conditions, but when the river is in flood they are a magnet to all fish species.

THE TREES

An overhanging tree is a magnet for all fish. It hides them from airborne predators, gives them shade on sunny days and there's the constant probability of insects falling from the leaves into the water and providing an easy meal. Fish also adore tree roots which enable them to get in close to the bank and feel completely safe. Therefore, the closer you can get your bait into the bank is very often the better.

THE BEAT BOUNDARY

Very often rivers are divided up into definite stretches or beats. Check your permit and make sure that you don't stray onto a stretch of river that you're not allowed to fish. The responsibility is yours.

THE ROCKS

All fish species adore rocks, as the rocks give them shelter from the current as well as sheltering a great deal of food items. Look for fish lying not just below rocks but also immediately above them. Rocks are particularly useful in high, fast water.

THE BEND

Find a bend on any river and you'll find fish. The current tends to slow on a bend and food drifting with the river falls to the bottom and is easy to find. Bends also tend to be deeper, especially on the bank where the current hits. Fish love this. There's often a crease on a bend – the point where faster and slower water meets. Work a bait down this crease because this is where most of the fish live.

THE INFLOWING STREAM

All main rivers will have their small tributaries, some just a trickle and some quite a major stream. All sizes are useful. They dribble in extra food stuffs and are very frequently used as spawning areas at certain times of the year. In times of flood, you'll often find that fish will leave the main river for the smaller side streams.

➤ THE BEAT BOUNDARY
As the sun sets and the angler comes to the end of his beat and of his day. He looks wistfully downriver thinking of water to be fished in the future.

THE BRIDGE
Bridges are magnets for both fish and fishermen. They give you height and allow you to look down into the river – perfect for fish spotting. Nearly every bridge has a downstream pool where the water is scoured out as the current squeezes between the pillars. Masonry from bridges gathers in these pools and provides protection from floods and harbours food supplies.

THE SHALLOWS
Every river will have extensive shallows, very often of gravel and sand. These are prime feeding areas, especially very early and very late in the day when the fish leave the security of deep water to move onto the food-rich margins. Barbel and chub in particular browse these shallows at dawn. Approach carefully and place a natural bait in their path.

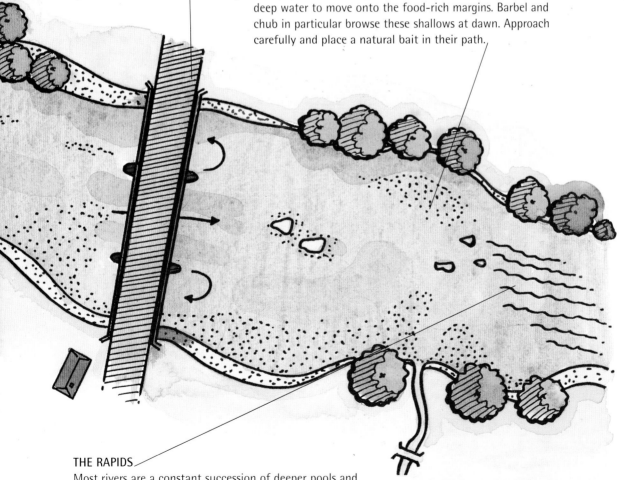

THE RAPIDS
Most rivers are a constant succession of deeper pools and shallow, fast-moving rapids. The rapids are especially sought after at dusk, through the night and at dawn because they're food-rich and the fish feel secure there. Rapids are also good in times of low flow and restricted oxygen.

STILLWATERS

It doesn't matter if you're fishing a farm pond, a lake or a reservoir, the same rules apply and the foremost one has to be location. No matter how good your bait or how excellent your tactics, if the fish aren't there in front of you then you're in for a boring session indeed. The most straightforward way of finding fish is simply to look for them.

Don't make the mistake of settling down in the swim handiest to the car-park. Leave your tackle behind, bar polaroid glasses and binoculars, and take the time to locate feeding fish. You could be catching within minutes of setting up rather than within hours.

What are you looking for? Often the signs are so obvious you can't miss them: a large area of muddy water, stained by fish rooting up the bottom; big patches of bubbles; the tail fins of fish upending in the shallows; large swirls on the surface or perhaps flat spots amid rippling water. If there's any sign of life or action, investigate it thoroughly.

Some signs are a little more subtle: you might just see some reeds twitching or a single solitary bubble rising to the surface. It could be that the surface of the water looks somehow unsettled. There's no obvious sign of fish activity, but the water just isn't moving in quite the right way. Follow up on hunches and you might well succeed.

⋎ IN THE FOREST
A seriously overgrown piece of water like this attracts fish for two reasons. Firstly, they feel secure amid lilies and overhanging trees, many of which have dropped branches into the water to provide further cover. Secondly, food stocks are often rich in the shallow, silty water that warms quickly in the spring.

➢ A HARD WON FISH
This cracking pike caused me quite a few problems. The major one, obviously, was to actually get to it. Chest waders were essential as they allowed me to wade out a long way from the bank, past the reed fringe that was far too dense to bring a hooked fish through.

Fishing the Margins

Let's say that you've found fish close in. This is always one of the most exciting elements of our sport and it can be heart-stopping stuff. In clear water, you can actually watch the fish take your very bait. You can even choose which fish you want to catch and target particular individuals, but it's never easy. You've got to be very careful in both your movements and the way you introduce bait. Generally, you'll just be loose feeding, scattering samples of the hook bait. Don't overdo this: it's better to keep the fish eager, rooting actively for food, than to overfeed them. Think carefully, too, about what you use. Bear in mind that pressured fish are often wary of light-coloured baits, so if you're using sweetcorn, for example, it pays to dye it either red or black. This is one reason why casters often prove more effective than maggots.

Think about how you are going to present your bait as well. Often a float offers the very best means of indication. Laying on, for example, is an old, tried and trusted method.

However, there is always one potential problem with float fishing – the line will inevitably hang from the float on its way to the lead and the bait on the bottom. Careful fish travelling in mid-water will pick up on this if it's clear and will make a definite detour. Any kind of float approach can therefore be more successful in murky water or at dawn or dusk. It you have any suspicions at all that the fish are seeing the line in mid-water then it pays to move on to a light leger and keep the line down low.

Fishing at short range means that you can get away with using very light leads indeed, so you're unlikely to scare the fish as your rig enters. The diagrams opposite show a couple of standard close-in rigs that

➤ TAKING CARE

Clive is taking absolutely no chances here. He's approached the water on all fours from a good twenty yards back and is making use of the boathouse pillars to break up his silhouette. The reason? There are three very big carp all over thirty pounds feeding in the shallows and he's well aware that any bankside commotion on a very quiet lake like this will immediately alert them to danger. His rod is all made up and he's ready to cast as soon as he's located the fish and got into position. Possible fault? Perhaps a hat would cast a shadow over his face and cut down any possible reflection.

⅄ LAY IT FLAT

When you're fishing very close you can think out your line of attack absolutely precisely. You can manoeuvre a bait as close as this – or even closer – to the lily pads where your line can be masked. Think, too, about your float. A cocked float in shallow water is like a beacon. It screams out danger. A float fished flat, however, is frequently less obvious.

are sensitive and will never tangle. You can use a quiver tip with them for bite indication but, in my view, a butt indicator of some sort is better. This gives a taking fish much more line and gives you that much more time to react positively.

Consider carefully whether you need to hair-rig or not. On pressured waters it's often necessary – the fish just won't pick up a traditionally hooked bait any longer – but if you can get away with side hooking a bait then do so. Using hair-rigs simply pushes fish up the ladder of knowledge more and more quickly and makes your task ever more problematic in the future.

⋎ CLASSIC BAITS

Maggots are an age-old bait and sweetcorn has certainly been around for more than 30 years. However, both still catch fish and they can be given a new lease of life if they're fished on a hair-rig like this. Try dyeing maggots and corn and giving them new, exotic flavours.

➢ THE MODERN BAIT

Boilies work with astounding efficiency for many species of fish, not just carp. It's becoming a tradition to hair-rig them but don't forget side hooking, which is simple and often effective.

Fishing Further Out

Often, fishing the margins isn't an option and the activity you see is taking place 30 yards out or even further. Arguably the most successful and straightforward method to use in these circumstances is the feeder/quiver tip combination. You can use either a block end feeder with maggots or an open-ended feeder with ground bait and samples of the hook bait inside. Superficially the feeder is a comparatively simple method but, of course, there are complexities. Make sure that your casting is tight and accurate. Don't cast the feeder into lots of different places because all you will do is break up the shoals of feeding fish. Line up a feature on the far bank and cast to it each and every time. Sometimes it pays to put a little piece of tape on your spool once you've cast out so that you'll be

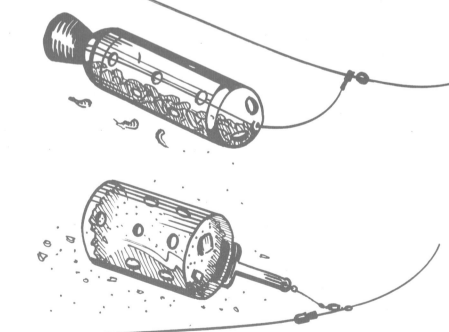

⋏ FEEDERS

Swim feeders come in all shapes and sizes, designed for use on both still and running water. The block end feeder (top) is perfect for maggots on any water. The other feeder (bottom) is open-ended and plugged with ground bait which explodes when the feeder hits the water. The feeder has the advantage of placing a carpet of bait very close to the hook, but in pressured water there are times when the fish become afraid of the feeder. Try a smaller feeder, or a different colour or shape.

◄ AUTUMN GOLD

Autumn can be a tricky time on stillwaters as temperatures begin to drop, clarity increases and, especially, surrounding trees begin to shed their leaves. As the leaves rot, they tend to thicken the water and turn the fish off the feed, but there's always hope. When the sun has started to set the fish will start to feed.

reaching exactly the same distance each time thereafter.

Consider your bites carefully: sometimes the tip will be pulled right round and you'll be left in no doubt whatsoever when to strike, but on other occasions the tip will merely flicker and nudge and you can't be sure whether these are line bites or the real thing. Experiment. Strike once, but if you don't hook up leave the next bite to develop. Experiment with your hook lengths. Go longer or shorter until you get positive indication. Change your hook baits around: try two maggots, then three maggots, then a maggot and caster combination until you find the answer.

The method feeder has made a huge impact on stillwaters over the last few years. It certainly attracts fish and, in heavily stocked waters especially, can prove irresistible. Remember, though, that you are casting out a comparatively heavy weight and you need to step up your

SUCCESFUL GROUND BAITING

Apparently choosing and preparing ground bait is now a highly technical process. We used to simply get a few sackfuls of stale bread, wet it, pulp it, squeeze it into balls and throw it out. Strangely, however, it often worked very well! Here are some basic tips.

• Mix your ground bait in a shallow, open bowl. Make sure the bowl is clean.
• The ground bait should be put in first and water added, little by little, until it begins to feel spongy and is easily moulded into firm balls.
• Take out small amounts, make them into balls and see if they hold together in the air and break up properly in the water at your feet. Once you're achieving the desired effect you can bait up your swim in earnest.
• Light ground bait, mixed less damp,

explodes much more quickly on impact. It should be wet enough to hold together in flight but soft enough to break down into fine particles on impact.
• For deep swims or fast-flowing water, a heavy ground bait mix should be used. Mix it fairly damp and squeeze the balls very tightly to increase the density.
• There are many commercial ground baits on the market, so choose carefully. Ask the dealer which ground bait is ideal for the water and species that you're targeting.
• Modern ground baits depend on taste, colour and activity. The ground bait must attract the fish but shouldn't frighten or overfeed them.
• When you're catapulting ground bait out, make sure your catapult cup is not one designed for propelling loose feed. It should be large and semi-rigid.

line strengths accordingly, or you risk snapping off on the cast. Bites tend to be very positive on the method feeder, so ignore the flicks and nudges of the quiver tip and wait for it to go right round. A couple of my own friends leave the reel on back-wind and don't even think of going to the rod until

they see the reel handle beginning to revolve. The method feeder isn't quite my cup of tea: I find it a little automatic, taking a lot of the skill out of stillwater fishing, but the fact remains that it is popular and it's effective, so we can't ignore it. The diagram below shows how it works.

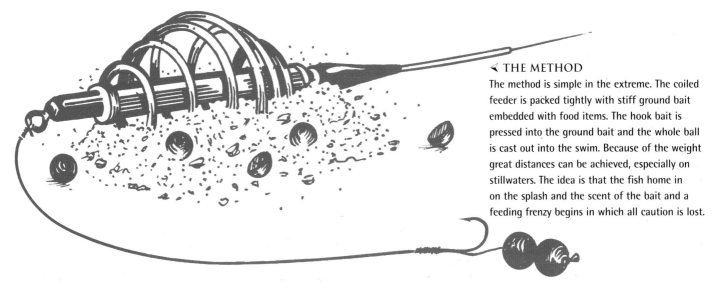

◄ THE METHOD

The method is simple in the extreme. The coiled feeder is packed tightly with stiff ground bait embedded with food items. The hook bait is pressed into the ground bait and the whole ball is cast out into the swim. Because of the weight great distances can be achieved, especially on stillwaters. The idea is that the fish home in on the splash and the scent of the bait and a feeding frenzy begins in which all caution is lost.

The Feederless Method

Traditionally, fishing at range meant mixing particles of bait in with ground bait and then catapulting the balls out to the desired spot. We hadn't thought of feeders back in the 1960s or early 70s but we still managed to catch fish, and on pressured waters it's a good idea to revert to methods that haven't been seen by the fish before. In essence, the method is almost exactly the same as using the feeder but you're catapulting the feed out rather than transporting it in the feeder itself.

What are the inherent problems with this method? Well, you've got to get your ground bait mix absolutely right. You don't want the balls to break up in the air and scatter all over the place. Similarly, you don't want to mix them like concrete so that they go in like miniature depth charges. The ideal

⋏ A SURFACE FEEDER

Watch the body language of a carp carefully when it comes up to feed off the surface. Only if it's moving slowly, happy to reveal a lot of its head and shoulders, is it likely to take a bait. Don't rush a surface feeder. Wait until you see all the signs of confidence before introducing your own hook bait. And then try to mask your line with weeds, reeds or fallen branches.

⋎ A FINE FAT FEMALE

Even though this tench was caught in the middle of summer, she's still holding a little spawn. So, notice how the hands are cradling her belly gently. We tend to think of tench baits as being on the small side – maggots, casters and the like – but this fish fell for a big impact bait – double lobworm, free-lined at 20 yards. The bite, however, was gentle.

is for them to begin breaking up
when they hit the surface and carry
on dissolving as they fall to the
bottom. This way you get a nice
three-dimensional effect and the fish
are pulled in by a constant curtain of
falling food. Maggots and casters are
perfect for this approach – casters
especially so, because some will
actually come free of the ground bait
when it hits the bottom and will rise
slowly towards the surface again,
increasing the visual attraction of
your area.

The whole secret to intelligent
ground baiting lies in attracting the
fish to the area and then holding
them there. For this reason, think
of using tiny particle baits, such as
grains of rice or hemp seed, that
keep the fish digging eagerly for
long periods of time. They can pick
up a few large baits and consume
them in minutes or even seconds.
A mass of particles keeps them busy
for hours.

As ever, there are downsides. Rice,
casters and hemp seed certainly
attract fish into the area, but
frequently bites are delicate and
small baits like this are difficult to
present. A hair-rig often becomes
necessary. If you're still having
problems, then abandon the particle
approach altogether and go for a big
impact bait like a couple of lobworms
on a size 4. This may be radically
different but it is often successful.

➤ USING THE DRIFT

Henry thought this approach out carefully. The
wind was pushing away from him, and from
his rocky ledge he was able to cast a piece of
bread a long way and then let the breeze do
the rest. He was able to work the bait to the
far trees on the right where he'd seen some
big fish swirling earlier. Playing fish from a
height gives you immaculate control and,
fortunately, there was a ledge beneath him
from which he could net a fish.

Fishing Without Ground Bait

Of course, all these latter methods involve a great deal of preparation and quite a weight of tackle and bait. This is fine for long, even multi-day, sessions but not so good if you want just a few hours of enjoyment. Don't be afraid of simply setting up a light rod, perhaps with a float, and using big impact, natural baits such as lobworms. If the water isn't obscenely crowded, simply walk round it and cast a lobworm into any likely looking spots. Fallen trees, extensive reed beds, close-in weed and manmade structures such as bridges and boat jetties all shelter feeding fish. Naturally, if you can actually see the fish themselves your chances are greatly enhanced.

Don't make the mistake of thinking that huge baiting routines are always necessary. It can often be that fish are alarmed by pre-baiting and much prefer to pick up a single,

⋏ A STALKED FISH

Dave is suitably proud of this fish. He'd seen it ghost in over shallows and he'd placed a hook loaded with sweetcorn in its path. The fight was brisk. Remember they don't all have to be 20-pounders to be acceptable.

⋎ ON THE QUILL

In this clear water Rob chose not to leger at range but to fish with a very large, very visible quill float. He could easily see it at 40 yards, rising the ripple, and bites simply buried it.

attractive food item – one that might have your hook in it. It would be wrong not to detail the more usual, modern approaches to stillwaters, but remember that it's always a good idea to think of your own approaches and even to buck the trend deliberately.

◄ A PRISTINE ROACH

Roach on any water can be baffling, but on big stillwaters they come and go like ghosts. Sometimes it is important to introduce a baiting programme, but at other times minimum feed helps your chances. On stillwaters if you can find areas of underwater tow you're at least halfway to catching the fish. Move along the bank with a small swim feeder, casting repeatedly until you find areas of real drift.

USING A FISH FINDER

I've already recommended in a previous chapter that you should think about getting afloat. If you have your own craft, or you are fishing waters where rowing boats are available, an electronic fish finder is an invaluable tool. Finders are a huge aid on large stillwaters especially. However, they are only a time-saver and not an infallible shortcut to putting fish on your hook.

• There are many, many models available now at a whole range of prices. Don't always go for the cheapest. Consider carefully what options you might require.

• Fish finders are tremendously useful, not only for picking out where shoals of fish, or large individuals, might be lying but also for giving you depth readings, pinpointing contours, weed beds, drop-offs and all the other features that could otherwise take you weeks to discover.

• If you're new to using a finder, spend half an hour over an area that you know very well. You can then collate what the finder tells you with what you already know about the water.

• Make sure that any machine you are thinking of buying is light. Often a long walk to a boat is required. It should be able to work off its own self-contained batteries rather than needing a car battery to operate it. Ideally, the recorder will be small enough to fit into a tackle bag like any other piece of equipment.

• Make sure the images on the screen are bright and sharp.

• One useful option is an audible alarm. This can be set to register sharp decreases in depth – very handy if you're on a large, rocky, exposed water with a risk of grounding.

• If you have a couple of fishing friends it makes sense to club together to buy a 'team' unit.

◄ PIONEERING A WATER

On a big water like this that you don't know much about it's imperative that you take your time to get to know it. Drive or walk round as much of the perimeter as you can, both looking for fish and studying the margins. Make a note of shallow bays and steep drop-offs. Look for places where woodland actually enters the water. Think about where the wind hits and where you've got areas of calm, placid water. If there are any anglers around pump them for local knowledge.

FISHING FOR PREDATORS

WHEN WE TALK ABOUT PREDATORS IT'S TEMPTING TO THINK ABOUT THE BIG BOYS ALONE – PIKE IN PARTICULAR. HOWEVER, IT'S WORTH REMEMBERING THAT MOST FISH TEND TO BE PREDATORY AT CERTAIN TIMES OF THE YEAR. EVEN CARP WILL STOOP TO PICKING UP A SMALL DEAD FISH FROM THE BOTTOM ON OCCASION AND IT'S NOT UNUSUAL TO SEE BARBEL HUNTING VORACIOUSLY FOR MINNOWS AND GUDGEON.

One of the beauties of predator fishing is that there are several lines of attack. For example, we can fish with lures, and what a world that opens up. Spinners, spoons, plugs, jigs, crank baits, jerk baits… an almost unending list of possibilities and opportunities. In fact, not surprisingly, there are anglers around the world who do nothing but fish with lures and enjoy every minute of it.

Fly fishing, too, is becoming an ever more popular way of catching predatory species, and why not? The fly behaves with stunning effect in the water, all fluidity and grace, as close an imitation to a natural, fleeing fish as you can imagine. Pike, for example, love flies and hit them hard. It's adrenaline-pumping stuff.

If you've got the patience and the time and you're prepared to sit it out for a single, possibly mighty, fish then you can also use dead bait. This isn't the most mobile way of fishing by any means, but it can produce the goods where other methods fail, and if your water is particularly cloudy, perhaps after heavy rains, then dead baiting may be the only one that works. There is much more to this technique than meets the eye: it's not just a case of whopping out a herring and sitting there until darkness enfolds you. There are all manner of different baits to try and different methods to employ.

Live baiting? Well, admittedly, it has been a top method throughout the years, but even a decade ago the quality of modern lures just wasn't available to anglers. My own view, and the view of countless thousands around the world, is that live baiting is now a method that we can do without. Live baits do catch fish, but there are all sorts of attendant problems and issues that make this a technique perhaps best consigned to the past.

➤ MONGOLIAN TRIUMPH
This fine taimen took a plug at a river junction. However, the scars on its back indicate that much bigger fish were present and this fish's tail was actually seized by another fish as the author was playing it to the bank.

◄ RUBBER BAITS
Jigs, rubber fish, jellies – call them what you will – they work splendidly. Not only is their action enticing but if a predator does get hold they feel much more natural than a plug or a spinner made from wood or metal.

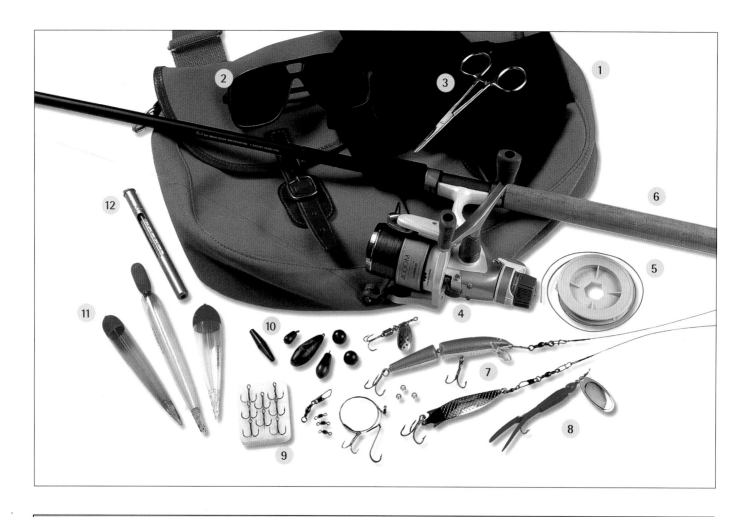

LURE FISHING EQUIPMENT

1 SHOULDER BAG *When you're travelling light this will carry all your gear.*

2 POLAROID GLASSES *These help you see the fish through the surface glare.*

3 FORCEPS *Forceps are necessary for removing hooks safely and easily.*

4 FIXED SPOOL REEL *A fixed spool reel is essential for trouble-free casting.*

5 TRACE WIRE *This is a must for all predators with sharp teeth.*

6 SPINNING ROD *Light and not too long, a good spinning rod should be comfortable and not too tiring on the arm.*

7 PLUG *A jointed plug gives out good vibrations as it wiggles through the water.*

8 METAL SPOON *A metal spoon has a good action in the water and catches the light. Note how both this and the plug are attached to a wire trace.*

9 TREBLE HOOKS *A selection of treble hooks for deadbaiting.*

10 WEIGHTS *Useful for taking a lure down deep in the water, and for anchoring a deadbait on the bottom.*

11 PIKE FLOATS *A selection of pike floats in various sizes to suit different waters and deadbaits.*

12 THERMOMETER *The temperature of the water can be crucial. If it is very cold then deadbaiting is likely to be more successful than a spoon or a plug.*

Lure Fishing

The enormous question is when and where to lure fish, and which of the thousands of lures on the market to use? Lure fishing can be practised at any time of the year in any weather but it does tend to be more explosive when the water is comparatively warm and, especially, fairly clear. If conditions are really freezing and/or the water is murky, then think hard about the dead baiting option, but let's say it's warmish, the lake or river in front of you is clear and you're just itching

➤ PERCH PARADISE

My old mate Bob James is checking out a lovely bit of perch water. It's got absolutely everything for the species. The deep water of the lock gates attracts them but there's plenty of cover around, too, from which they can mount an ambush. Look at the exuberant bed of rushes to the left and the overhanging trees on the right. In the clear water, Bob can see fish taking small fry whenever they venture out into open water.

to get lure fishing. So where do you start?

Location is the key. When you're lure fishing you can't really pre-bait and draw the pike to you, so you've got to search them out. Pike, large or small, tend to hang next to cover, as this gives them security from bigger fish and allows them to mount an ambush on passing prey fish, so look for reed beds, lily pads, islands, bridges, fallen trees, dumped human rubbish, anything that breaks up the normal pattern of the water. I once found a lovely pike nestling in an old supermarket trolley! Think about underwater contours – sudden drop-offs or depressions often

harbour fish. Are there any in-flowing streams, perhaps?

Think also about the time of year. In spring, when pike are beginning to spawn, they'll move into shallow bays where the water warms quickly. Later on, they are also quick to capitalize on spawning prey fish, so it pays dividends to keep your eye on what is going on in the water as a whole. Pike enjoy basking in warm water, so if it's a hot, sunny day you will almost certainly find them near the surface,

perhaps moving slowly in and out of the shade of lilies. As winter approaches and the water cools, you'll probably find the pike in slightly deeper water, sliding away from the margins where cold nights begin to have an impact. Pike will often group together when they're patrolling and actively hunting, so if you catch one fish it makes sense to stay on in the area and search out others. Always keep your eyes open: a carpet of scattering fish almost certainly means that a pike, or even a group of pike, is very much on the prowl. Get yourself into the area as quickly as possible. Look for the duckling that's snatched, for the water rat that dives but never comes back up. In winter, search out the remnants of weed beds or watch where the grebe is diving. It's feeding on shoals of small fish that will probably attract fishy predators as well. Be alert to everything that's happening around you and you will find that your catches rocket.

◄ IN THE STICKS

Look at this stickleback and you'll see why perch rarely move far from snags of one sort or another. Sticklebacks, minnows and fingerlings all realize that their very lives depend on being as invisible as possible, and you don't get to live long by swimming around in open water.

The Simple Spinner

So what kind of lure should we begin with? If you suspect that the water in front of you is full of small pike, then a simple silver spinner a couple of inches long is probably all you're going to need throughout the day. Pike of up to seven pounds or so will take these with reckless abandon, and there's probably nothing they prefer in your entire box. You can catch big pike on tiny spinners but, by and large, the larger the fish the more you're going to have to experiment. Every year there are millions of words written about lure fishing, but the fact remains that there are no hard and fast rules, and even experts learn every time they go out, so

don't be afraid to try everything, no matter how bizarre it might seem.

Let me give you an example: some years ago I was fishing in Mongolia for particularly large and cunning pike. Nothing worked for me, but a Czech further down the bank was having stunning success. He was casting out a big silver spoon and letting it hit bottom. He would then twitch it back a yard at a time, letting it grub along the bottom and then lie static for anything up to 30 seconds before pulling it on its way. Imagine the impact this was having down there… the bottom suddenly erupting with puffs of silt… a crippled, silvery shape scuttling along the bottom, looking for cover,

obviously terrified. As the wounded creature comes nearer, the dozing pike begins to stir, its fins start to work, its body trembles – and then the spinner is gone, the rod is hooped over, the reel is singing and an impossible method has proved that everything is possible in the world of lure fishing.

▾ FINELY MARKED
Once again, let me stress that no fish needs to be a monster to be appreciated and this small perch is a perfect example of what I'm saying. In this day of modern lures it is easy to forget the old favourites, but small Mepps spinners like this have worked well for generations, so don't discard them. You'll sometimes find that a different coloured blade works wonders when simple silver or gold draws a blank.

I ought to explain about this box of plugs. They were created by a Czech friend of mine for taimen fishing in Mongolia. They replicate as nearly as possible the lenok trout and baby taimen upon which the big fish feed. And they're tremendously successful. This raises a big question. How lifelike should your lures be? Are you trying to imitate small prey fish exactly or give an impression of how they look and behave? Perhaps it is best to leave no stone unturned: use a lure that looks right but, above all, make it work right.

The World of Plugs

Plug fishing is, to a degree, more complex just because there are so many different designs, shapes, colours and working actions to be taken into account. Possibly the most exciting of all plug fishing is on the surface, and there's a vast variety of creations to choose from. Jitterbugs, Crazy Crawlers, Buzzing Frogs – even the names get you excited! Use surface plugs around weed beds or under overhanging branches, and really search out the vital ambush points. Some surface lures have built-in action supplied by lips or blades and others have a built-in body action that make them twitch as you retrieve to impart a darting action. You can buy 'weedless' surface lures on which the hook has a weed guard to keep it from fouling up. Try these for fishing right over lily pads and dense weed beds where pike are resting up but where other lures can't be used. Surface lures are often successful in warm weather, when the pike are eager to chase a food source. Pike not only see them but they feel their vibrations as well: jumping and splashing, popping through the water with propellers creating a wake, surface lures churn out an impossible-to-ignore message to hungry fish.

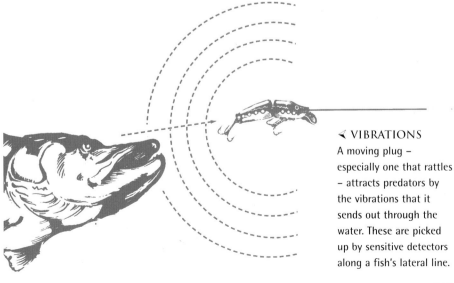

◄ VIBRATIONS
A moving plug – especially one that rattles – attracts predators by the vibrations that it sends out through the water. These are picked up by sensitive detectors along a fish's lateral line.

◀ JOINTED PLUGS
Plugs come in all sorts of shapes, sizes and colours. Jointed plugs, which have a 'lip' to make them dive, often have a very dramatic wiggle indeed. When retrieved slowly they look just like a wounded fish – and an easy meal.

◀ THE COPPER SPOON
Spoons are one of the oldest forms of lures. Their curved shape makes them wobble and flicker as they move through the water. Very enticing to any big predator, especially on a sunny day when the light catches the polished metal.

◀ THE FLYING CONDOM
There's something about the Flying C that makes it irresistible to many types of predatorial fish.

Even in hot weather, though, not all fish are near the surface and often the bigger ones will be down deeper. This is where you need to use diving plugs. The angle of the 'lip' gives a clue as to how deep plugs will dive. The bigger the lip and the deeper the angle, the greater the depths a plug will investigate for you. Jerk baits are now a major part of the angling scene world wide and they have a big reputation, especially for deeper water fishing. There's nothing fancy about jerk baits. You are working large, sometimes monster, baits that are carefully made and balanced to cope brilliantly with the deepest fishing. In the hands of a skilful angler they really leap to life.

To get jerk bait fishing right, go for a stiff rod designed for the purpose and a solid leader that will avoid tangles for you. A braid line helps ensure that the action you impart through your rod tip is transmitted all the way down to the lure and isn't softened by the stretch of nylon. Then it's up to you. Really work that rod tip. Crank down fast to rip the jerk bait down

deep. Let everything go still, so that it rises with an enticing wobble – and see what happens.

Choosing the correct jerk bait for any particular job can be confusing. The main consideration is the depth of the water you'll be fishing in and the level where you think the fish are feeding. For this reason, it's important to know the sink rate of every jerk bait in your box. For example, if it's cold and you're convinced the pike are really down deep, go for a jerk bait that sinks perhaps a yard per second and can really get down to where the fish are lying.

Think, too, about colours. If the water is very murky you need to use a plug that is brilliant and flashy. For example, I've done well with big goldfish lures when the water has been like chocolate. Hot Tiger is another good colour in stained and murky waters. When visibility is less than a couple of feet I go for fluorescent or white or the shiniest silver, but you can never tell. Out in India the guides swear by big, silver lures when the sun is high. They think these catch the sun's rays and

bounce them out, pulling the big, predatory mahseer in irresistibly. On the other hand, big trout up in Scotland often only pursue black lures on days like this. Maybe it's the way the fish are lying, or the silhouette of the lure through the water. Perhaps we'll just never know. The message is simple – if you're not succeeding, keep on trying something different.

The size of a jerk bait or normal plug is also important. You can use mini-plugs for all manner of predatory fish – use them just the length of your little finger for chub, perch, asp or black bass. You can go huge – a foot long or more – if you're after a monster pike, musky or Mongolian taimen.

➤ RUBBER CAUGHT
This fish was hugely important to me. It was caught by a Swedish friend and was about his thirtieth of the morning. I had caught nothing. Not a take. I'd been using my standard plugs on a bay in the Baltic and drawn a blank while my companion had had fish after fish on rubber. That was years ago and obviously I learnt the lesson. In clear water especially, rubbers are often the best way forward.

The Art and Nature of the Jig

For me, there's no more exciting way of lure fishing than using jigs, and they're certainly incredibly adaptable. A jig is a simple concept that uses a large, single hook with a lead head moulded round its eye. You then impale a soft, plastic body shape upon the hook. The size of the lead head is important because it determines how deep the jig will work. The plastic body is vital. These come in endless combinations of shape, colour, size and action.

⅄ CAUGHT IN THE LIGHT

It sometimes takes a stroke of luck to produce a take. For example, you can be working a jig like this daylong and then suddenly the sun squints from behind the clouds and illuminates it with a piercing glow. A predator that's shown no interest for minutes can unexpectedly be spurred into a violent attack. That's why it is important to keep going, to keep your spirits up and not give up if the going seems tough.

Some are like snakes, others frogs, others small fish… it's a fantastic world of the most sinuous, supple forms. A jig is ideal for working along or near to the bottom, and it's especially useful when times are hard, perhaps in cold or coloured water conditions when the fish are reluctant to stir far. Jigs are totally versatile and you can retrieve them in mid-water, vertically or even trolled behind a boat.

My own favourite jigs? Well, I love rubber crayfish for black bass… let it twitch its way through the water to the bottom and then pull it slowly back in short, scuttling motions. I love all the shad patterns for good-sized pike. Make sure the rubber bodies are tough enough to resist the attention of innumerable sharp teeth, but pliable enough to give a realistic action and to feel natural when a

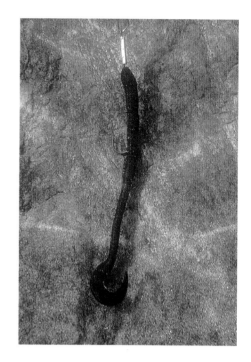

⅄ WRIGGLING

Think carefully about where and how you fish a jig. This worm looks absolutely fantastic inched up an underwater rock face. It's the sort of lure that could be taken by virtually anything from bass in freshwater to a wrasse in the sea.

◄ GETTING IT RIGHT
The hooking and weighting of jigs is all-important. If your hook isn't big enough or isn't positioned properly you're going to miss bites. If the lead head, as it's called, isn't heavy enough then you're not going to get the jig down properly and it's not going to work with the right sort of action. Experiment with different hooks and lead heads and watch how the jigs work in the margins at your feet. Don't start fishing seriously until you're quite happy everything is spot on.

fish picks it up. Look carefully at the hook on the lead head. It needs to be sharp – absolutely essential for jig fishing – but also really strong, because you could be talking big fish here.

Go for a wide selection of body colours. Predators are frequently really particular in their choice of lure and they'll change their preference from day to day. As a very rough guide, in gin-clear water start out with natural patterns such as roach or rainbow trout. If the water is slightly more cloudy, look for patterns that have stripes or bars along them. Fire Tiger is a good starter here. If the water is coloured, then contrasting patterns and colours often make an impact. If the water is really clouded, then go for vibrant colours and, above all, jigs with a really powerful action that sends out shock waves through the water for the fish to pick up on.

Remember that the deeper the fish, the heavier the lead head you will need to keep in contact. Think about the currents, which can lessen your contact and make the jig work

less effectively. Try jigging vertically, especially if you're in a boat, letting the jig rise up and flutter back towards the bottom. Consider, too, the effect of bottom weed: if your jig is constantly coming back cloaked with dying vegetation it won't be working effectively, so go for something a little lighter.

⅄ WORKING THE WATER
The great bonus about lure fishing is that you can really work the water and keep on the move until you locate fish. Mind you, a really hard day can be punishing on the muscles and on the back especially. It's often a good idea to strap yourself up with a back support, particularly if you're wading as this tires the body even more. Make sure, too, that your clothing, which should include a hat, totally insulates you from the wind and the damp.

Pike on the Fly

If you're going to join the ever-expanding band of pike fly fishermen then you'll need the right gear. Pike flies are generally hefty articles several inches long, and they demand powerful tackle for safe casting. Generally you'll be going for about a 9-foot rod that takes a 10-weight line. This is meaty gear, but it's necessary. Anything less and you just won't have the control over a big fly like this. It's not just a matter of casting: you also need to set that hook. Always use wire traces with your flies, and these shouldn't be too short, especially if you think there could well be big fish about.

When you're starting out in this branch of the sport, it's probably best to go to a shallow, comparatively clear, well-stocked water in warm weather. You'll need action to build up your confidence, and if you're experiencing endless blanks you can't really know whether you're making progress or not. Cast your fly into all the places that you'd put a normal lure: holes amidst the weed beds; close up to reeds; on the fringes of overhanging trees. Watch out for small fish scattering, and for big angry swirls on the surface. If you can wade, great. If you can get out in a boat, even better.

A lot of big trout reservoirs are now allowing pike anglers on them providing they use flies. This is a more specialized business. Here you'll be looking at sinking lines to get those big flies down to much greater depths. You'll need to have some idea at what depth the pike are lying and how long it's going to take your fly to reach them. An electric fishfinder is often a wise investment if you're embarking on a really demanding challenge such as this.

➤ FRUITS FROM A HARD DAY
Ian deserves great credit for this catch, as the fishing on this cold day was particularly difficult with lures and dead baits. Ian decided to put up his fly gear and the result was this small but very welcome pike. It is good to remember that if the weather is cold, fly success is ever more likely as the water warms.

➤ EYE-CATCHING PIKE CATCHER
This dramatic streamer fly is a real pike catcher. In the water it ripples and flows just like the real thing. Experiment for yourself: pull a fly like this back through the margins close to your feet and you'll see exactly how real and languid it looks. Notice the single hook – kind on the fish because it is easy to remove – and study that hefty, uncompromising piece of trace wire.

Dead Baiting

Freezing weather. Chocolate waters. Low pike populations, but big fish present. The chances are that you will have to use a dead bait. The choice is huge, and probably the most effective baits are dead sea fish: mackerel, herring, sprat and sardine are all very effective. Sardines, however, are very soft, so unless they are frozen you won't be able to cast them long distances. You don't need to go to the fish mongers, because many other dead bait types are now commercially available: eel sections, lamprey, pollan and various dead freshwater species can also make excellent baits, especially if the pike aren't used to associating them with danger.

You can also make your baits even more attractive by dyeing them, scenting them or even packing them

with polystyrene so they float up from the bottom. If you're comparatively new to the game then my advice would be to present your dead baits under a float, simply because takes are much more easily seen that way. A pike will very often just sidle up to a dead bait and sip it in gently with no need to bolt off, giving an unmissable take. Even the biggest fish might only dip the float a couple of inches, so be constantly

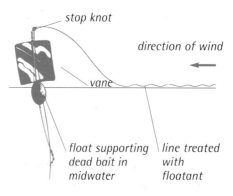

stop knot

direction of wind

vane

float supporting dead bait in midwater

line treated with floatant

⋏ PICKING A DEAD BAIT
Remember that on any specific day one type of dead bait will be ignored whilst another will be picked up. If you're not having success on mackerel then try herring. If that fails, go to freshwater fish and if they fail try eels or lampreys and so on. Just because dead baiting is a more static type of fishing than using lures it doesn't mean to say that your brain switches off. Keep it in gear. Keep thinking. Keep searching. You will catch fish if you're lazy but you'll catch a whole lot more if you're industrious.

◄ THE DRIFT FLOAT
This rig works well when searching out large waters when there's a decent breeze blowing. The vane catches the wind and will trot before it, providing the line is well-greased, covering huge areas of the water. It is quite possible to drift the float over 150 yards or more, but it's wise to have binoculars with you at these distances so that you can see a take. Once the float disappears, wind down tight and strike immediately to avoid deep hooking.

➤ A SERIOUS REWARD
These two photographs represent a truly successful piece of fishing. There was cascading rain and winds well above gale force that sometimes actually lifted the line, float and bait clear of the water, but Alex and Rob stuck it out. That's the key. If you're going to be a serious predator angler then dress appropriately and kick into the right mindset.

aware. If you are going to leger a dead bait, make sure your set up is absolutely spot on and will register any pick-up immediately.

Think of putting your dead bait in exactly the same places that you'd work your spinner, fly or jerk bait. Look for dying back weed beds, overhanging trees and all the usual ambush points. However, considering that dead baits are a really big fish method, it also pays to search out deeper channels and depressions where monsters frequently lurk. If the water is totally unknown to you, keep mobile. Don't let your dead bait lie for more than half an hour, and move on if it goes unmolested.

If there's a breeze, set up a drifting rig (see diagram). This allows you to explore vast chunks of water that are simply too far out for you to cast to. One important point when using the drift rig is that you must watch the float acutely, through binoculars if necessary. If you're fishing at 150 yards range, it takes time to see the bite, wind down and strike. If you're not paying attention the bait could be down in the throat, and everyone wants to avoid a deep-hooked pike.

The New Attitude

There was a time when predator fishing, and pike fishing especially, was considered dull work. Pike were fished for almost exclusively in the winter, and clothing in those dark days was pitifully inadequate. Now, because of the use of thermals and breathable waterproofs we are

nowhere near as tortured by the weather. Also, because of the great strides forward in jigs, jerk baits and especially plugs, we have a whole new range of methods that can catch pike whatever the conditions and keep us interested and active as well. Even dead baiting has made huge strides over the last few years. Different types of dead baits and different ways of presenting them all make life much more fascinating than it once was. The true predator angler today has a really enquiring mind and is aware of the scores and scores of approaches to catching his favourite type of fish. No longer is it

⅄ AN INTERESTING FISH
This was an interesting water. It seemed that nearly all the fish apart from the very large ones were suspiciously thin. The conclusion reached was that there were few prey fish in the water but that the very big fish got fat by eating the young of their own species. We were later to receive partial confirmation of this theory by catching a number of very good fish indeed on jack pike imitation plugs.

a case of simply drowning a mackerel, picking up a good book and nodding off under an umbrella. The modern predator angler is a master of experiment, a fisherman willing to learn all the new crafts that are being pioneered.

CARP FISHING

Today, the carp is an international species found on every continent and pursued by enormous numbers of anglers. The chances are there will be plenty of opportunities for carp fishing wherever you are based, and you must make your own mind up about the level at which you want to begin.

Carp can be very difficult if they're big, pressured and thinly scattered through a large water. Equally, they're quite catchable if they're heavily stocked in a smaller water where locating them isn't a problem. The choice is pretty much up to you, but it's probably better to begin on easier waters, build up confidence and experience and then move on up the ladder as your confidence increases. Here, I'm going to describe approaches to both small and large waters. I'm assuming that the carp are reasonably difficult in both and I'll look at the major problems that you're likely to face.

Carp in Small Waters

By small, I mean carp waters that are anything from half an acre in extent up to about 10 acres. These are not puddles, but they're manageable and you shouldn't be put off by their sheer scale. Always start by walking slowly and carefully round a water of this size. If it's absolutely ringed with anglers, then you will be pushed into one of the few swims available, but on many waters, especially at unfashionable times of the year, you're likely to have a lot of bank space to choose from. Use that choice wisely. Look carefully for any signs of feeding fish… all the usual ones: stained water, bubbles, suspiciously moving weed, twitching reeds, the sight of fins or backs. If you don't see any sign of fish, look carefully for places they might want to live. These include areas close to snags, areas that are hard to reach, perhaps around islands or under overhanging trees… in fact, anywhere that a carp is likely to feel secure and comparatively unthreatened.

Baits and Pre-Baits

If you have areas of water to yourself, it's a good idea to pre-bait a few spots before even putting up your tackle. Take your bait with you as you're walking the lake and wherever you see either fish or a spot that screams fish introduce some samples of your hook bait. If you can, throw the bait out by hand, but if the fish are further out you'll need a catapult. As for the choice of bait, well, boilies are

➤ WELL ON THE FEED
Careful thought with your baiting can really pay dividends. Try to lay down a carpet of food that the carp will really like. Choose the colours, flavourings and scents with great care and you could have a gold rush on your hands!

◄ AMERICAN CARP
This beautiful common carp was caught on a fascinating river in New York State. Bass were the target of all the locals and the carp, beautiful as they were, were totally ignored.

obviously the norm, but don't be shackled by them. Consider dyed sweetcorn, maggots or casters if there are not too many small fish around. Carp pellets are excellent and so, too, are all manner of nuts and seeds. Soaked peanuts, for example, are a great bait. They can be injurious to the carp when introduced in huge quantities, so don't think of a colossal baiting campaign, but a handful here and there should do no harm.

ᐁ TRICKS OF THE TRADE

You'll have learnt from reading this book that I'm a great advocate of getting to know the fish, their habits, their environment and then approaching them in as simple a way as possible. Generally, I truly believe this is the right way but I freely admit that carp can be a case apart. Carp do learn and they're long-lived and so you've often got to be one step ahead of their own personal game. You're helped in this by the carp industry itself. This is hugely inventive and there are vast numbers of truly pioneering anglers always developing new techniques and the tackle necessary to go

with them. We're looking here at one – and I stress one – of the tackle boxes of my friend Peter. Just think about his braid hook lengths. Different diameters, different colours, even camouflaged – anything to give him the edge. It's the same with leads – different sizes, different shapes, different colours and, again, if necessary, camouflaged. You might have a favourite pattern of hook, too: however, odds are you'll need many different patterns if you're going to cope successfully with different situations. But don't panic. Carp aren't super-beings and experience will soon teach you the right way to go.

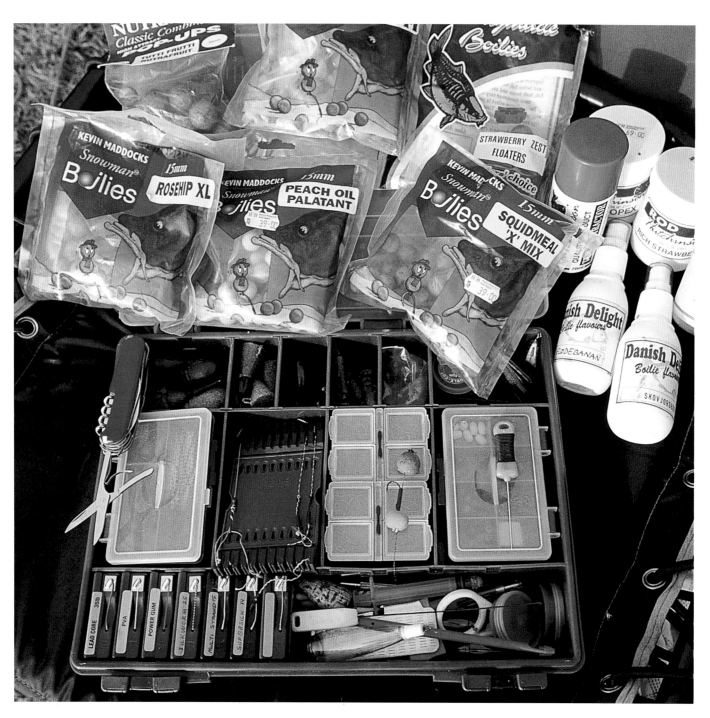

You must have confidence in your baits, and if you can pre-bait in a few areas it's not a bad idea to mix and match. For example, try maggots and casters in one area, coloured corn in another, pellets in a third and different particles or boilies in the remainder. Hopefully, you can then gain some indication of which baits are coming out on top.

While on the subject of baits, I'm a great believer in big impact baits –

those baits that carp look at and simply can't resist. Making a decision doesn't come into it: they just have to have them. Very often big impact baits are naturals – two or three big lobworms on a size 4 hook, for example, especially after a heavy summer downpour. Big black slugs can be good and you might even try a large moth or Daddy Longlegs in warm weather when the fish are slurping in the surface film close in.

⅄ MODERN BAITS

Boilies have dominated the carp fishing bait scene for 20 years and for good reason. The fish love them and you have a whole world of scope to experiment with different colours, flavours and sizes. Don't neglect other developments either. The various carp pellets work tremendously well – often better than boilies themselves in hard-fished waters. And don't forget particles: these were pioneered a quarter of a century or more ago and are sometimes overlooked. Even sweetcorn has its uses if it is dyed and flavoured or if the fish have totally forgotten about its existence and its dangers!

Be Prepared

You've got to be on top of your tackle and methods if you're fishing close in to snags on small waters. You must hit a fish as soon as it's taken the bait and really power it away from trouble, or you will lose carp after carp. This means your indication has to be spot on and your gear has to be up to the job. When it comes to indication, floats can be excellent: you know exactly where your bait is going to be, and very often in shallow water you will see the carp working up close to it. This means you're ready and prepared. Whether you use float or leger, don't be hesitant after the strike. You've really got to turn that fish's head out into open water in the first two or three seconds or the game can easily be lost. Don't let a carp work up speed, as its weight will then be given added momentum and the task will become ever more difficult. If you can keep stopping a carp in its tracks you have a much better chance of landing it in tight places.

Small water carping is great for intimate fishing and allowing you to see exactly what's going on. If you're not catching fish, then you can often

actually see what mistakes you're making. For example, fish are very frequently afraid of line hanging in mid water. If they are, it could be that a float isn't the right answer and you'll have to go for a lead, keeping the line well down on the bottom. A back lead, too, can be a good idea, ensuring there's no line wavering around to scare fish. Alternatively, it could be that the carp don't like the look of the float itself: make no mistake, they are eagle-eyed and

anything alien can be spotted. So, if long casting isn't necessary, why not substitute the commercial float for a stick or even a discarded swan or goose feather? These are quite natural and will ring no alarm bells.

Fishing tight like this often allows you to place your bait and gear as inconspicuously as possible. For example, if there's bright sunlight, try to get your terminal tackle deep down amongst weed or branches in the shade where it will be less conspicuous. Alternatively, lie your terminal tackle on the very edge of a dense weed bed where, again, it will blend in much more encouragingly.

Be bold. Try a number of approaches. You don't always have to night fish, but you will find that very

first light tends to be a strong feeding period, as is dusk. Try fishing without any pre-baiting whatsoever: sometimes a bed of bait can set off the alarm in a fish's mind and a single, acceptable, well-presented bait can be much more willingly taken. Alternatively, mount a real ambush and put a bait in a small clearing that you know fish visit every now and again through the course of the day. Cast out, clip up and simply sit the thing out. Chances are there'll be lots to watch up and down the waterside to keep you interested. Don't be afraid of fishing inches out from the margins: you'll often find carp with their bodies almost against the bank itself searching for food that's drifted in on the breeze.

Keep checking the water out. Just because you went to the shallows at 2pm, say, and saw no fish it doesn't mean that carp won't have moved in by 5pm. Binoculars can often help by allowing you to scan more of the water and getting round the need to get up close and possibly scare the fish. Look for those small, sheltered bays where the wind has pushed scum and surface floating food. These will often fish particularly well in the evening. A natural bait, like a dead moth or cranefly, can work very well presented either on the surface or just underneath.

◁ JOHNNY GETS TO WORK

Carp feed day and night and this fish woke up my great pal Johnny in the early hours of the morning. However, just because numbers of fish are caught nocturnally, don't for a moment think that's the only time that they're approachable. It's not. If you fish during daylight hours – even on hard-pressured waters – you'll find carp eager to feed.

On the Surface

Wherever you fish, always introduce some floating baits at some point during the day because you might well be able to get fish to the surface, which is the most exciting way to catch carp. Dog and cat biscuits are among the most popular floating baits. Pouring boiling water over them for a couple of minutes can soften them. Flavours can be added by aerosol, but don't overdo the flavour until you're sure that it's working. Pieces from a large crusty loaf can be just as good. Experiment with the sizes: sometimes a piece the size of your palm will work, whereas at other times you've got to go down to thumbnail-size.

Position yourself on the bank where the breeze is behind you and either throw or catapult some samples out into the wind channel. Watch them carefully as they blow down the lake and in all probability you will soon begin to see some backs, swirls, heads and even open,

▲ THE HUMBLE CRUST

Surface fishing really began well over half a century ago and in those days anglers pretty much only used bread. Then we entered the age of the dog and cat biscuits and bread has largely been forgotten, but carp still love bread. Other small fish enjoy it as well, and clouds of fingerlings under a piece of flake soon attract a big fish into the area. Always go for a fresh, crusty loaf.

▼ HAPPY TO FEED AT ALL LEVELS

This carp has come into a shallow bay where it is feeding hard on bloodworm. It stirs the water up and colours it in its exertions but a smelly surface bait may well still attract it. Carp can get preoccupied on small food stuffs but they're opportunistic feeders and a large, attractive surface bait such as this hunk of bread will soon catch its attention. It's also a lot easier to fish than microscopic bloodworm.

sucking mouths. Don't be in too much of a hurry to cast out, rather let the fish build up confidence before you introduce the hook bait.

Make sure your presentation is as neat as possible. Keep mending the line to prevent a big bow from developing. This will only catch the wind and skate the biscuit across the surface in an unnatural fashion. It's not a bad idea to actually sink the last foot or two of line up to the bait to make it less conspicuous. A controller float helps you to see bites and to control the biscuit in its drift but, on hard-fished waters, the carp may be wary of this. If so, tie on a bit of twig, preferably with a couple

of leaves standing proud. The carp won't suspect a piece of vegetation and the leaves will catch the wind and help the bait on its journey out.

Don't think you have to use floaters in open water alone: watch carefully where the untaken baits finally wash up on the windward bank, perhaps in bays, under fallen trees or amid marginal weed. Here large, careful carp will often glide in and take freebies all but unnoticed.

All these small-water tactics call for two major qualities: firstly, keep calm, confident and in control. Don't panic if you suddenly find a big fish coming towards your bait; keep thinking, and success will be on your

⋏ RELAXED FISH

Here you see part of a clutch of fine common carp photographed relaxing on a warm summer's day. You might think these fish are thinking about anything but feeding, but something tempting presented to them in a non-threatening way will almost invariably be sipped in. Try something just sub-surface – an air-injected worm for example. Or go for something natural – a big Daddy Long Legs is always likely to be sucked in. They will also go for artificials just as much as the real thing.

side. Secondly, this is eyeball-to-eyeball fishing, so carefully consider your camouflage skills. Move slowly, dress in drab colours and talk quietly. The slightest movement could undo hours of ambush effort.

▲ DEFYING SCIENCE

If you read any of the textbooks, you'll find that the maximum size for comizo barbel – the fish featured here – is given at seven or eight pounds! Multiply that figure two or three times and you're getting nearer the mark. That's the beauty about fishing these very large waters – you might end up with the carp of your dreams or a stunning fish like this.

Fishing the Larger Water

A medium to large water can be anything from a 15-acre pit to a lake or reservoir 10 miles long or more. The major problem to overcome when fishing such waters is lack of confidence. Where on earth do you start? Well, if possible, view your water from an elevated position. Try to walk or drive round as much of it as possible. Talk to local carp anglers… not all are secretive. Talk to local pleasure anglers who are after so-called lesser species. They might have seen carp crashing about and will be able to give you tips. Think which way the predominant wind blows. Generally the shores that face it will be the most productive, although not always, and least of all in winter when the winds are cold. Look for any features that can focus your attention: islands, plateaux, gravel bars, reed beds, weeded areas, inlet streams, boathouses, dam walls, water towers, deep troughs, large rocks… anything, as I say, that breaks up the huge expanse of water before you and allows you to focus.

It's a mistake to think that on big waters carp are always found miles out. The larger the water the less pressure there is likely to be, and this means that carp will often come in close. Look especially for shallow bays. These are food-rich and they also warm up quickly – and carp love to bask. If you find carp in a bay, then pursue them with just the same tactics I've already described for the small waters.

Setting Up

The chances are that you'll want to tackle your big water with a multi-hour session, perhaps for a few days, so you'll need to set up base camp. The first and over-riding decision is where to bivvy up with a good chance of finding fish. You might go, for example, where a lake narrows so that you're sitting on a good ambush point. Set yourself up comfortably, but don't destroy vegetation. Be very careful with fires if the bank is tinder dry and never leave litter. There

◄ VIRTUALLY A NECESSITY
On large waters the ability to get afloat can make a huge amount of difference to your success rate. A boat often makes transporting gear up and down the lake easier, especially to inaccessible points and headlands. Vitally, a boat allows you to bait up with supreme accuracy a long distance from the shore. Also, if a big fish becomes weeded or snagged then with a boat it is still possible to get the thing out, whereas your chances are slim indeed if you're stuck on the bankside.

⚘ MARKING THE SPOT
If you put bait out a very long way it is often difficult to know exactly the location if you're 100 yards from it on the bank. This floating buoy goes over the side of a boat as you bait up so that when you get back to the bank you'll know exactly where to cast.

should be no sign of your presence once you've gone.

Now to the all-important part of getting your bait out. On a really large water the odds are that your hook bait will be boilies, but choose carefully and, once you've made your decision, stick with it and show confidence. You can get your boilies out either by catapult, spod (see page 125), throwing stick, radio-controlled boat or perhaps an inflatable that you can row out yourself. It's often a good idea to make exploratory casts beforehand to make sure that there are no unexpected snags or weed beds. You can also plumb the depth to make sure that it's what you expect.

How much bait do you put out? This largely depends on the length of your session, the size of the water and the head of carp you believe to

exist. The bigger the number of fish and the larger the size of the fish, the more bait you should introduce. The weather also makes a difference: carp tend to feed harder when the water is warmer. To put it simply, there's just no easy answer to this one. I suppose I would begin with a bucket of boilies – say about 2 gallons. I would probably introduce this over a bed of particles of some sort, something like maize – quite cheap and cheerful. Obviously, if you do have access to an inflatable boat this speeds up the baiting process no end. In fact, you

can get two or three bucketfuls of bait out in a matter of 10 minutes or so. If you're forced to do the job from the bank, allow a couple of hours before everything is ready.

If you're fishing at range – say 50 to 150 yards – then you will need to put a marker out to pinpoint exactly where you want to cast. Once again, a marker is best deposited from a boat. Once you've got your required casting distance, it's a good idea to put a bit of tape over the spool at this point so the length of each cast is exactly the same.

➤ LANDED
Peter and Rafa are justifiably pleased with this lovely looking fish, which they most certainly would have lost but for the access to Peter's inflatable boat. The fish had snagged itself in a long, sunken tree branch and only direct pressure from above saved the day.

Terminal Tackle

Now we come to the all-important question of rig. Above all, try to keep your rigs simple. Don't go for glamour rigs that are overly complicated until you're absolutely sure that you need them. The more complicated the rig, the more likely it is to tangle in flight, especially over long distances. If you're sitting behind a couple of baits for 20 hours or more you need to have complete confidence that there's no mess up at the rig end.

Do you use nylon or braid? Braid has an incredible diameter-to-strength ratio and is very limp, but don't use it if you're fishing close to rocks or snags because it abrades quickly. Do you need a shock leader? You certainly do if you're casting very heavy leads and baits long distances on comparatively light line. Try to develop your casting techniques. Most anglers use the direct overhead cast, but don't rush it – build up the power gradually. A snatched cast is a cast that will go astray. Position yourself

comfortably before the cast and make sure that you're happy with your rod and your reel – you can't cast 100 yards plus if your gear just isn't up to it, and if you strain for extra feet then your technique will suffer and accuracy will be sacrificed. Indeed, it's best to fish comparatively close in for your first few sessions and build up the distance gradually as your confidence and expertise increase. Even when you really are competent at fishing 120 yards away, don't always assume you need to. Casting at the horizon is often unnecessary and you could actually be fishing way over distance.

Look carefully at all the photographs on these pages because they will give you some clues when it comes to different approaches. Remember to think things out for yourself and don't just go with the latest gimmick. In fact, on very large waters you generally don't have to be quite as cunning as you do on smaller waters, simply because the fish are likely to have

⋏ PEST PROOF

This took some believing, for me anyway. It's a rig commonly used on large European waters where crayfish and, believe me or not, terrapins are bait-thieving problems. The concept is an easy one. You simply put the boily in a small, plastic cage which keeps it safe from prying claws and beaks. But, obviously, you'd think it would keep the boily pretty well safe from the mouth of a carp too. But not so. In fact, sometimes the success rate is actually enhanced by the use of a cage. Strange, I know, but true.

faced less pressure. Choose your bait and your method, and build up a real relationship with them. You'll find that you form a happy partnership and will be able to take them onto other venues with complete confidence.

Confidence is a key word here. If you're constantly worrying about your rig and your bait there's a temptation to be continually reeling in to check one or the other. Experiment until you find a set of rigs that work for you in different situations and then really stick with them.

CHOOSING AND USING A SPOD

A spod is a rocket-shaped tube designed to be cast out to carry free offerings of bait to your desired fishing area. The spod has a float at the pointed end so that it lifts and spills the bait out when it hits the water. It's a good, quick, accurate way of baiting up an area. It tends to be used specifically by carp fishermen using boilies, but other baits can also be spodded.

• Choose the spod carefully. You'll need a bigger spod if you're casting larger baits or longer distances.

• It's worth investing in a specifically designed spod rod. These are cheap but they do the job very well.

• You'll need a big reel with strong line so that you don't snap off on the cast.

• Fill the spod three-quarters full of bait.

• Dunk it in the lake to fill it to the top with water. Don't reel the spod too tight to the rod tip, and try to cast with a smooth pendulum-like motion. A snatched cast will wobble the spod and spill the bait.

• Try to hit the same target again and again. Tie a piece of power gum onto your main line so you know exactly when to feather and stop the cast.

• When the spod is about to hit the water, jolt the rod back very slightly so that it slaps on the surface as opposed to shooting deep into it. You'll find the bait comes out better like this.

• Wait until you're sure all the bait is emptied out. It's truly annoying to reel in and find there's still bait in the spod.

• When retrieving the spod, try to lift the back end out of the water and reel it in as quickly as you can. This skims it across the surface making reeling much easier and less intrusive.

⊼ A PVA SOCK

If you haven't been able to lay out a carpet of bait or if you're beginning to suspect that it's dwindling fast because of heavy feeding, then it's very useful to get a scattering of free offerings close to your own hook bait. The best way of doing this is through a PVA stocking like this. Depending on the length and diameter of the stocking, you can often put out 50 or more boilies, so if you're working two or three rods this makes for a significant baiting programme. The package isn't particularly aerodynamic but the weight allows you to make the distance provided your rod, reel and line are up to it.

⊲ THE BUSINESS END

Notice how Peter attaches the stocking to his terminal tackle. There's little or no chance of it spinning off in flight and in the warm water the PVA will melt very quickly indeed. You can see that Peter is using a double boily bait here. On really large waters with big, relatively unsophisticated fish you can stretch to three or even four boilies for a quick-fire pick up.

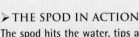

➢ THE SPOD IN ACTION

The spod hits the water, tips and spills its content of boilies down into the chosen area. This is a great method of baiting up at extreme range, but after the large splashes that the spod creates don't expect an instant reaction from the carp. Often it will take a good few hours – perhaps even a day – for this area of the water to settle down and the fish to become less suspicious.

◀ A TEAM EFFORT

Tim wields the rod and Kerry holds the net as a lovely fish rolls into sight. This carp was actually caught at range in the mouth of a major bay. However, look at that ridge of coloured water that stretches a rod-length out from the bank. This was created by a heavy onshore breeze that disturbed the silt and sand to create a coffee-coloured stain. The carp proved quick to respond to this and shortly after this shot was taken whole groups of fish were seen working the margins for the food released. This is the point about big waters: they are very dynamic, always changing, always volatile. Keep your eye on them and monitor changing conditions constantly.

Playing Your Carp

When you do hook big fish at range, it's important to take control quickly. If you fail to conquer a fish hooked at 120 yards, you can soon find yourself playing it 200 yards away, and that really does become a problem, so keep on top of the fish and keep pumping it back towards you. At long range, the chances are that the fight will be quite spongy, and you've really got to watch out when the fish begins to near the shallows, as it will start making long and heavy runs.

In reservoirs, especially, you'll often find areas that are very snaggy indeed. Perhaps you're fishing close to old submerged buildings or even the remnants of felled forest. Fish can easily find sanctuary in snags like these and it's good, if not imperative, to have a boat available

⋏ AFTERCARE

If you must take your fish from the water for accurate recording purposes then use a wetted unhooking mat. Watch the fish carefully lest it wriggle off and damage itself on surrounding stones or gravel.

⋎ KIND TO THE FISH

It is preferable for fish to be photographed in the water. Wear chest waders and kneel with your fish in clear, shallow, safe lake margins.

so that you can get out there and exert vertical pressure. However, don't go out in the boat in bad weather, don't go out at night and don't go out at all if you're not a strong swimmer. Always use a buoyancy aid, and make sure you've got friends on the bank to help you in any sort of emergency.

Think about the well-being of your carp as well. A long-range battle is necessarily time consuming and the fish is likely to be very tired and stressed by the end of it. If you're fishing in hot weather or in a hot country then recovery periods are likely to be longer in oxygen-depleted water. Try to keep the fish submerged as much as possible and

make sure any photographs are done quickly and close to the waterline. Always use a very soft unhooking mat and don't let a carp drop onto hard rocks or parched grass. Support the carp in the margins for as long as it takes before its strength returns and it's ready to make its own, relaxed journey back to the deeps.

Remember that even on very large waters there aren't always huge heads of fish. You might find that the shoals are large – often two or three hundred strong – but that doesn't mean to say that these rafts of fish are spread everywhere throughout the water. Frequently there can be hundreds of yards, if not miles, of barren lake between

them. So it really does make sense to look after the fish that you're catching to ensure that you have sport well into the future.

➤ A GREAT DANE

Johnny Jensen, seen here holding a fantastic carp, is one of the best anglers I know. It's partly down to experience, but his preparation is always immaculate. He pays great attention to the quality of his bait and exactly the right terminal rig to use in any situation.

⟶ A COMMON DELIGHT

Peter at it again, nursing a lovely fish. It was an opportunist capture: while he had his rods out at range, he noticed a pod of fish coming into a bay to feed and a couple of grains of sweetcorn under a float accounted for this 20-pounder.

TIPS FOR THE LONG SESSION CARP ANGLER

Long sessions demand a bit of planning. Don't go into them ill prepared.

• If the weather is cold, make sure you've got ample warm clothing and your sleeping bag is up to the job – even warm days can be followed by cold nights. If the weather is blisteringly hot, make sure you're not out in the open sun for too long. Heat-stroke is a real problem, and can be doubly so if you're a long way from medical aid. Keep yourself well hydrated with mineral water. Avoid alcohol, as this dehydrates you further and can increase the effects of sunstroke.

• Ensure your bivvy is on level ground. If you're having problems sleeping, your fishing abilities will gradually decrease as the session develops. Don't turn a long-stay session into a stressful experience.

• Ensure that you've got enough food and that you eat regularly. Use a camping stove to cook rather than lighting a fire.

• If you're out in the wilds, tell people exactly where you're going and when you expect to be back. Stick to your timetable or at least phone to prevent anyone sending out a search party.

• Don't bivvy up alone on remote waters. If you're injured, help can be very difficult to summon, especially if you're out of mobile phone contact.

• Always make sure that you've got plenty of bait with you and plenty of spare kit. There's nothing more frustrating than being forced from the water by the lack of something essential.

• Take plenty of entertainment with you – books or magazines, and perhaps a radio. It's a good idea to keep a diary.

• Binoculars can help you enjoy the wildlife as well as looking for moving fish.

• Don't be blinkered by the long range stuff but keep your eyes on what's happening along the margins. Keep two or three areas regularly baited up and approach them cautiously every few hours to see if there are fish feeding there. An unexpected whopper could come your way quite easily.

• Tidy up meticulously when your session is over and don't leave a scrap of litter. Make sure any human waste is comprehensively buried.

FLYING FISHING

IT WOULD BE WRONG NOT TO END BY TALKING ABOUT THE TWO BIGGEST DEVELOPMENTS IN THE FRESHWATER-FISHING WORLD. THE FIRST IS THE EVER-INCREASING USE OF THE FLY FOR ALL SPECIES, NOT JUST SALMONIDS, AND THE SECOND IS THE RECENT PHENOMENAL GROWTH IN ANGLING TRAVEL. TWENTY YEARS AGO FRESHWATER FISHING WAS ALL ABOUT BAIT IN THE BACK YARD, BUT NOT TODAY.

I hinted at the growing importance of fly fishing in the predator chapter when I urged you to think about taking up a fly rod for pike, but what makes fly fishing so good? Well, I firmly believe that fishing should be fun, that it should be all about having the best time of your life, so I feel anything that increases the pleasure you derive from the sport is truly to be applauded – and that's where fly fishing comes in. It's just a beautiful way of fishing. Learning to cast is a joy in itself – put out a sweetly-singing fly line and it really doesn't matter whether you catch a fish at the end of the cast or not. The simple physical pleasure that you can derive from purring out 30 yards of line is very frequently enough.

What's more, fly fishing brings out the very best of the fisherman-naturalist in you: in no other branch of the sport is it more important to observe what the fish are feeding on and try and imitate it to the closest possible degree. Fly fishing really strips away the veil between you and the fish, and you begin to see with brilliant clarity what you're trying to achieve.

Lastly, and best of all for me, fly fishing means that you can travel supremely light. You don't bother with boxes or seats, with buckets of bait, with umbrellas, rod rests or any of the usual trappings of the traditional freshwater scene. Rod, reel, line and a box of flies – that's it. You're free to travel and explore as

 FISH ON

All types of fishing are great but none come better than this. A river warm enough to wade in shorts. A beating sun. Birds all around and a distant otter calling. And then a fish takes a fly. You zip tight, the rod keels over and the reel shrieks in your hand. Okay, you've been a bait fisherman all your life but don't, for goodness sake, cut yourself off from the fantastic experiences a fly rod can bring.

◄ TRIBUTE

I'd like here to pay tribute to a great friend of mine Mike Smith, a fishery owner who died just a few years ago after a bravely battled illness. Mike was in the vanguard of enlightened fishery management. His lakes were thoughtfully and carefully run. Stocking levels were never too high but fair both to the angler and to the fish. The lakes were immaculately kept. Mike knew everything about both his stillwaters and, importantly, the delightful stretch of river that meandered through his fishery. It was in this that his pride and joy lived: a freely-breeding stock of wild brown trout. He would purr with contentment over his 30-pound carp but then absolutely drool over the beauty of a fin-perfect 8-ounce brownie. Mike with his humour, generosity and profound knowledge will always be missed.

much bankside as you're physically capable of walking. You're unfettered. The water is your oyster. Go and enjoy it all.

As I see it, the world of fishing is changing fast, and plenty of old boundaries are melting away. Fishing is, or should be, full of all manner of pleasures, excitements and challenges. The rigid carp fisherman who refuses to trot a float for roach, jig a lure for pike or flick a fly for trout is missing a lot. The tweedy colonel who won't fish for anything but salmon is also missing out in a big way. I have to say that it's in the UK that these divisions are, even today, at their most rigid. Americans, Scandinavians, Germans… here are anglers knowledgeable in many disciplines and open to them all.

Of course, fly fishing is traditionally seen as the method for the salmonids – for trout, salmon and perhaps grayling in particular – and this is indeed fantastic sport. The waters are frequently peaceful and beautiful, and you're often pursuing wild fish. There is an impression, again certainly in the UK, that such fishing is always expensive, but this isn't necessarily the case. There's a great deal of water throughout the world that can be fished for next to nothing, and you don't need a millionaire's bank balance to enjoy top sport.

Remember that fish don't have to be huge to be hugely appreciated! If

➢ STREAM WORK
Don't forget that often you hardly have to cast out at all. All over the world there are tiny little streams like this where it's all about the creepy-crawly approach and tight, pinpoint flicking of the fly. And you'd be surprised how large some of the fish are in tiny waters like this. In New Zealand, for example, streams no wider than this can produce trout of ten pounds or more. Of course, these are old, wary fish and just have to be returned. But then, shouldn't all wild fish go back?

you want big fish all the time then, yes, it's going to cost you money. However, biggest isn't always best, and a small, wild, natural fish is often more highly prized than a large, clumsy, stocked one.

CASTING A FLY LINE

1 GETTING STARTED
Hold the fly in your left hand while you pull some line off the reel. Then flick the line and the fly into the water.

2 PULLING LINE OFF THE REEL
The next step is to pull a yard or so of line off the reel. Shake the rod so that this line runs through the rings.

3 REPEAT THE PROCESS
Pull off more line and again waggle the rod so that it follows down through into the water. You'll now have enough line out to start a cast.

7 GETTING READY TO GO LONG
The first short cast is completed and the extra fly line can be seen clearly now hanging beneath the reel.

8 GOING FOR A LONG CAST
The line is picked up off the water as the rod goes backwards. Let the extra line go through your fingers.

9 KEEP YOUR EYE ON THAT FLY
You've now got about ten yards of line behind you. For the first cast or so look behind to make sure that the line straightens properly.

4 FALSE CASTING
False casting is all about moving your rod backwards and forwards as you get more and more fly line out into the air.

5 START SHORT
After one or two false casts, let the fly land seven or eight yards in front of you. There could be a fish close into the bank.

6 MORE LINE OUT
At the end of this first short cast, pull more line off your reel – about another two yards or so.

10 OUT IT GOES
On your forwards cast, the whole ten or 11 yards of line shoots out and lands gently in the river before you.

11 A STEADY RETRIEVE
As the fly swings round in the current, keep the line tight by pulling in any slack with your left hand.

12 STARTING OVER
You've now got quite a bit of line in your left hand and you're raising the rod to cast again. Keep everything smooth and controlled.

Investigating New Horizons

More and more, the traditionally bait-fished species that I've talked about at length in this book are being targeted by fly-fishing techniques, and not just predators such as pike and perch. For myself, I feel I'm making real headway with barbel on the fly. Chub are known fly takers. Roach and tench will also come to a nymph. In the wider world there are few more exciting targets than asp and bass, for example. I'm quite sure that it's in this whole arena that the real new fishing discoveries of this century will be made. Over the past decades we have only scratched the surface. I predict that within 20 years it will be just as normal to fish for bream on the fly as it is now with maggots and ground bait.

Another relatively new development that's rapidly gathering pace is the use of fly tackle in the sea – and why not? Let's keep on blurring the boundaries. Okay, you can go exotic and fish the 'flats' of Florida, the Bahamas or the Seychelles for bonefish, permit and barracuda, but when the winds and tides are right you can also fish more northerly waters for sea bass, mullet, wrasse, pollock and mackerel. This is really exciting sport: the fish fight like demons and, of course, you're talking now about fishing that is nearly always absolutely free.

Let's take on board several things: firstly, fly-fishing tackle does not have to be expensive. In fact, it can be a great deal cheaper than virtually all bait-fishing gear. Of course, you can spend a vast amount on rods and reels if you choose, but a good, standard, entry-level outfit can come in at around the price of an average feeder rod.

Nor is casting difficult: it's like learning to swim or riding a bike – it's a knack, and as a competent angler you will soon find it easy to master. I would say that within four or five hours an average bait fisherman will be casting a fly with some degree of confidence. Of course, it makes good sense to go to a casting instructor at least a couple of times: perhaps before you begin and then after a month or so, just to make sure you're not developing any mistakes. For a serious angler, many of the other difficulties melt away. You're already in tune with fish and the waters they live in. You're already aware of the subtle importance of changes in weather and light. In truth, you're a proper fisherman, not a learner, and you'll find you will take to fly fishing like a duck to water.

If you want to take this idea up, you may like to check out *The Complete Guide to Fly Fishing*, my companion book in this series. You'll see how straightforward fly fishing is and how there's absolutely no need for you to fear its supposed intricacies and complexities. Do a bit of reading, some watching, a little talking, spend some time practising and you'll be a fly fisherman before you know it – and exceedingly happy to be so.

◄ NEW ZEALAND GLORY
You just won't find more beautiful trout rivers anywhere in the world than those of New Zealand. They are gloriously unpolluted and brimful of wild, perfectly-conditioned fish. Mind you, they're not easy: the water is generally crystal clear and New Zealanders nearly always operate a policy of catch and release, so the fish do wise-up.

➤ SPANISH DELIGHT
Fly fishing on a Spanish river in the late spring when the flowers are blooming, the water is clear and the barbel, bass and trout are feeding hard. No wonder Bob looks and feels as though he's in paradise! Notice Bob's crouching stance and the concentration he puts into casting. Even though he's vastly experienced he wants to land the fly with pinpoint accuracy and feather-light impact.

Flying Fishing

You have several options in your fishing life. You can stay local, fish your home waters and get to know them absolutely intimately. This is a good approach – it's satisfying and you do become an expert. You can choose to travel a little more adventurously within the confines of your own country. Again, this is fun, and it pushes you just a little bit further. You meet other experts and expand your own knowledge. You look forward to your trips away: even if they're infrequent and comparatively short, they're still exciting and will give you a new slant on what you're doing in the rest of the year.

This could well inspire you to make a bigger adventure, to leave your country altogether and travel to another, probably within the same continent. This is where things really get exciting: you'll find yourself in a different culture, you might experience different weather, you'll probably be listening to a different language and very likely be pursuing different species of fish. You'll find that methods are quite, quite different: sometimes those you know will work exceptionally well and you'll make the locals sit up and think. At other times, you'll be knocked out by the methods that they're using and you'll be itching to take them home and adapt them to your own waters. Your mind is in turmoil. You never thought there could be so much to it.

In fact, you could be so thrilled by the whole experience that you decide to go in for a mega trip and take a long haul flight to a totally different continent. Wow! This is when your world is truly turned upside down. The lives you see around you are so completely different to the one you lead at home. The waters, too, are absolutely unrecognizable. They're probably larger, or deeper or hotter. The fish species seem unbelievably exotic and it's not until you actually see them for yourself that you can really believe that they exist! You find the locals have ideas that you would never have dreamed of on your own. They may be living in huts with no electricity or sanitation, but they possess fishing skills you can only marvel at. When the time comes to head home, as it does all too quickly, you travel back not just a changed angler but a different person.

Yes, fishing really can have this impact on your life. For me and for many of my friends, there's been no more potent influence.

⋏ ABSOLUTELY WONDROUS

Even a man as tough as big Bob, from the wilds of British Columbia, can only gawp at a steelhead, a sea-running rainbow trout, as wonderful as this. Of all the fish I've caught in well over forty countries of the world, pound for pound, nothing fights like a steelhead straight from the sea. They display a gallantry that's almost insane, a bravery that's heartbreaking.

⋖ TAKE TO THE SEA

Sea fishing need not be crude or heavy handed, and most of it isn't. When you come to the flats of the tropics in search of grey ghosts like bonefish it truly becomes one of the most absorbing of all aspects of fishing. Bonefish come and go with the tides. They may be small but they fight like jet-propelled rockets. Fidel, in the foreground, is an absolute magician at seeing fish and catching them, when to the rest of the world they seem impossible.

⋗ IT'S A WONDERFUL WORLD

And here I am in the autumn sunshine basking in the view of eastern Mongolia and the Chinese border. A vast, lonely, unspoilt paradise where the fishing is probably as exceptional as it was a thousand years ago. The internal combustion engine has a lot of bad things to answer for but at least, because of it, we can enjoy the privilege of being in such places.

A World of Possibility

Where would I rate the biggest adventures of today? Well, in Asia I'd place Indian mahseer, Mongolian taimen and Russian catfish as absolute musts. In Australasia, who can ignore the barramundi, the huge New Zealand eels and the fantastic brown trout fishing? In North America you have everything – steelhead, sturgeon, muskies, carp fishing beyond your dreams, fantastic pike fishing, king salmon, fabulous steelheads and lake trout that make European ferox look like fingerlings. In South America you have hundreds of Amazonian species, including peacock bass and the almost legendary arapaima, as well as the extraordinary sea trout of the Falklands and colossal wild rainbows

in Argentina. In Africa, there are the real behemoths, the Nile perch, which grow to an incredible size. There are also tiger fish and, only to be spoken of in hushed tones, the Goliath tiger. In all probability, this last species is restricted in its range to the Congo Basin, which means danger and deprivation… and that's just getting to the fishing. So few anglers have ever caught Goliaths that the literature on them is skimpy in the extreme. This is true pioneering action.

You can see what a world there is out there for the angler. It's immense. It's neverending. Let it unfold before you like a magic carpet and allow it to take your life to places beyond your dreams. Believe me, you'll never regret being a fisherman.

➤ AND FAREWELL
This is how I like to see all fish treated. Magnus holds a bonefish towards the open sea, a creature that he has hooked and landed without ever removing it from its environment. A magnificent fish in a magnificent setting. This photograph is what the wonderful fishing world is all about.

ⅴ DINOSAUR FISH
Believe it or not, this was the smallest sturgeon my friend Johnny and I caught in an entire week when some 60 or 70 fish were landed. The sturgeon is, arguably, the oldest fish on Earth today – a real fossil of a fish and, tragically, threatened by the greed of mankind for its precious black roe, the caviar. It's just possible that sport fishing and the hard currency it brings might save these creatures from extinction by poachers.

GLOSSARY OF KNOTS

I T IS ESSENTIAL FOR EVERY ANGLER TO KNOW HOW TO TIE A SELECTION OF KNOTS. KNOTS ARE USED TO SECURE THE LINE TO THE REEL AND TO JOIN A HOOK OR LURE TO THE LINE. ALTHOUGH THERE ARE THOUSANDS OF DIFFERENT KNOTS, THE BASIC KNOTS ILLUSTRATED BELOW WILL BE SUFFICIENT FOR ANGLING PURPOSES.

HALF BLOOD KNOT

The half blood knot is commonly used for joining hook to line. This type of knot, when tied in nylon line, will not come undone.

⚓ STEP 1
Thread the free end of the line through the eye of the hook.

⚓ STEP 2
Pass the free end underneath the line and bring it back over the line to form a loop.

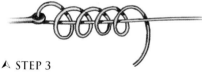

⚓ STEP 3
Continue to loop the free end over the line (as step 2) until you have approximately four turns.

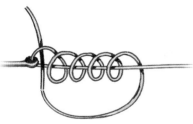

⚓ STEP 4
Pass the loose end between the eye of the hook and the first loop.

⚓ STEP 5
Pull on the loose end to tighten the knot. Trim off the end.

DOUBLE OVERHAND LOOP

Also known as the surgeon's loop, this knot can be used to create a loop at the end of a fly line to which a looped leader can be attached.

⚓ STEP 1
To begin, double the end of the line back against itself.

⚓ STEP 2
Next, tie an overhand knot in the doubled line.

⚓ STEP 3
The doubled end should then be tucked through the loop again.

⚓ STEP 4
To finish, pull the knot as tight as possible and trim off the end.

BLOOD BIGHT

This knot has similar properties to the double overhand loop. If the end of the knot is not trimmed, several loops can be created to attach, for example, mackerel flies.

⚓ STEP 1
Fold the end of the line back against itself (this is known as a bight).

⚓ STEP 2
Cross the the doubled end once round the line.

⚓ STEP 3
Pass the looped end of the line back through the turn.

⚓ STEP 4
Pull the knot tight. Trim off the end of the line to finish.

WATER KNOT

This knot is also known as the surgeon's knot. The water knot is used to join two lines together, for example attaching a lighter hook length to the mainline. The bulk of the knot will stop a sliding bead and can be useful when legering.

⋏ STEP 1
Put the ends of the two lines alongside each other so that they overlap by about six inches.

⋏ STEP 2
Take hold of the two lines and make a wide loop.

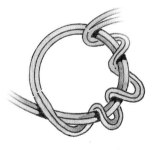

⋏ STEP 3
Pass the ends of the line through the loop four times. Be sure to hold the two lines together.

⋏ STEP 4
Pull the lines tightly so that the loop makes a knot. Trim the two ends.

BLOOD KNOT

The blood knot is also used to join two lines together. As in the water knot, begin by overlapping the ends of the two lines.

⋏ STEP 1
Take one end and twist it four times round the other line. Then pass it between the two lines.

⋏ STEP 2
Repeat with the other free end. Make sure that the first stage does not come undone.

⋏ STEP 3
Wet the knot to lubricate it, then pull it tight. Trim off the two ends.

NEEDLE KNOT

The needle knot shown here can be used to tie solid monofilament to a fly line.

⋏ STEP 1
Push a needle through the end of the fly line, Heat the needle until the line begins to bend.

⋏ STEP 2
When cool, remove needle. Thread the mono through the fly line and five times round it. Bring the end back and hold it against the line.

⋏ STEP 3
Now take the large loop and bring it several times round the fly line, trapping the mono.

⋏ STEP 4
Pull on alternate ends of the mono to tighten. When the knot is firm, pull the mono tight.

A BRAID LOOP

Although some fly lines are fitted with braided lines for attaching a leader, it is a simple task to form your own from braided mono.

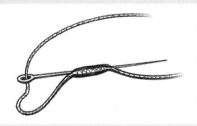

⋏ STEP 1
Push a large-eyed needle into the braid. Thread the braid through the eye.

⋏ STEP 2
Push the needle through the braid until the loose end emerges. A matchstick will keep the loop from closing.

⋏ STEP 3
Adjust the loop until it is the size you require. Cut the loose end until it lies flush, and seal using waterproof superglue.

INDEX

Page references in *italics* indicate illustrations.

ACKNOWLEDGEMENTS

As ever, please let me thank Johnny Jensen from Copenhagen and Martin H. Smith from Norfolk to whom I know I owe so much in terms of friendship and photographic fishing, help, encouragement and advice. Without your support guys I'd be even more feeble behind the camera than I am now!

I count myself hugely fortunate that I now seem to have a raft of fishing friends around the world. It's almost invidious to pick out any of them for fear of offending those left out. There are hundreds of men and women of all races and colours who have helped me with ideas along the way. It would, however, be wrong not to pick out Rob Olsen, the illustrator of this book and truly one of the best five anglers I have ever encountered. His skill is only matched by his sensitivity. Having mentioned Rob perhaps I can also throw out such names as Phil, Alan, John, Peter Smith and Peter Staggs, Mick, Leo, and Ian, as well as both Saad and Anthony Cruz who make my Indian expeditions the joy that they have become.

I'd like to thank Jo Hemmings for her continued support throughout the years, Andrew Easton and Kate Michell for performing so sterlingly and, above all, Carol Selwyn, without whom not a single word of this book would ever have appeared.